FamilyFun
Super Snacks

125 Quick Snacks That Are Fun to Make and to Eat

DISNEP
EDITIONS

NEW YORK

FamilyFun Super Snacks

FAMILYFUN

EDITORS
Deanna F. Cook
Grace Ganssle
Alexandra Kennedy

EDITORIAL ASSISTANTS
Laura M. Gomes
Jean Graham
Amy Hamel
Heather Johnson

COPY EDITOR
Faye Wolfe

CONTRIBUTING EDITORS
Mary Giles
Gregory Lauzon
Cindy A. Littlefield

CONTRIBUTING WRITER
Catherine Newman

PICTURE EDITOR
Mark Mantegna

PRODUCTION
Jennifer Mayer
Dana Stiepock

TECHNOLOGY COORDINATOR
Tom Lepper

IMPRESS INC.
CREATIVE DIRECTOR
Hans Teensma

DESIGN DIRECTOR
Carolyn Eckert

DESIGN ASSOCIATE
Katie Craig

PROJECTS DIRECTOR
Lisa Newman

ART ASSOCIATES
Jen Darcy
Katie Winger

This book is dedicated to the readers of *FamilyFun* magazine.

All of the ideas in this book first appeared in *FamilyFun* magazine. *FamilyFun* is a division of the Walt Disney Publishing Group. To order a subscription, call 800-289-4849.

The staffs of *FamilyFun* and Impress, Inc., conceived and produced *FamilyFun Super Snacks* at 244 Main Street, Northampton, Massachusetts 01060, in collaboration with Disney Editions, 114 Fifth Avenue, New York, New York 10011-5690.

Special thanks to the following *FamilyFun* magazine writers for their contributions: Barbara Beery, Cynthia Caldwell, Sharon Miller Cindrich, Toybe Cook, Amy Cotler, Teresa K. Edmiston, Ken Haedrich, Amy Hamel, Mollie Katzen, Frederick G. Levine, Julia Lynch, Elaine Magee, Charlotte Meryman, Catherine Newman, Leslie Garisto Pfaff, Jodi Picoult, Susan G. Purdy, Kathy Schultz, Edwina Stevenson, Emily B. Todd, Penny Warner, Deborah Way, Stacey Webb, and Lynn Zimmerman.

We extend our gratitude to *FamilyFun*'s many creative readers who shared with us their snack ideas. Thanks to Tawni Ballinger, Kathleen S. Bostrom, Janet Bricault, Christine Crytzer, Kerri De Ruiter, Mary Anne DeZur, Rebecca Edwards, Debbie Fohr, Susan Freeman, Susan Herbert, Shelley Kotulka, Brenda Lindsay, Rachel and Jacob Meyer, Patty Miller, Keith Millner, Lori Murray, Lori Nienau, Mary Patten, Dot Price, Emily Pulvermacher, Ericka Purtee, Kate Romero, Jane Stark, Nancy Wallace, and Tracey Watson.

This book would not have been possible without the talented *FamilyFun* magazine staff, who edited and art-directed the recipes for the magazine from 1993 to 2004. In addition to the book staff credited on the previous page, we'd like to acknowledge the following staff members: Jonathan Adolph, Douglas Bantz, Nicole Blasenak, Kristen Branch, Jodi Butler, Terry Carr, Dawn Chipman, Barbara Findlen, Moira Greto, Michael Grinley, Ann Hallock, Ginger Barr Heafey, Elaine Kehoe, Laura MacKay, Adrienne Stolarz, Mike Trotman, Ellen Harter Wall, Sandra L. Wickland, and Katharine Whittemore. We also would like to thank our partners at Disney Editions, especially Wendy Lefkon and Jody Revenson.

ABOUT THE EDITOR:
Deanna F. Cook, Creative Development Director of *FamilyFun* magazine, is the editor of the *FamilyFun* book series from Disney Editions, as well as the author of *The Kids' Multicultural Cookbook* from Williamson. She cooks in her Florence, Massachusetts, home with her husband, Doug, and their girls, Ella and Maisie.

ISBN 0-7868-5424-3

First Edition
10 9 8 7 6 5 4 3 2 1

Library of Congress Cataloging-in-Publication Data on file

Contents

Tortilla Chip Strips, page 37

It's Snack Time

A SNACK ATTACK can sneak up on your kids at any time. When they're just home from school, on their way to karate, or even raking leaves on a weekend morning, you may hear the sudden "I'm starving!" that signals its onset. The kids need food — and they need it fast. But with snacks accounting for a significant portion of our children's daily caloric intake, we don't always want them grabbing for packaged snack foods — the kind that offer lots of crunch but little nutrition.

It's time to take these mini meals seriously. Well, maybe not too seriously. The recipes you'll find in the pages that follow have many things in common, but seriousness is not among them. Instead you'll find dozens of snack activities that are as fun — and as quick — to make as they are to eat. From the zany Bagel Critters (page 57) and the showy Vegetable Flowers (page 24) to the yummy Peanut Butter Bugs (page 68) and mini Pizza Muffins (page 49), our kid favorites will satisfy every craving — and they're all made with ingredients you already have on hand. We also offer "Kids' Steps" with every recipe (to encourage those budding chefs), nutrition tips, time-savers, preparation times, and great snack ideas from the readers of *FamilyFun* magazine — all you need, in fact, to make that "fourth meal" one that really counts.

Enlist a young chef. Kids love to help, and a snack makes the perfect training ground. A kitchen project also lets you and your child spend time together while dinner cooks. And if it's your family's turn to bring a snack to school or a scout meeting, your child will be proud to have made it himself.

Let them play with their food. Many of these recipes, for Fresh Fruit Pizza (page 15) or the simple Green Bean Serpents (page 28) for instance, are so interactive that they make great after-school activities as well as great snacks. We supply the ideas, you supply the edible craft materials, and your kids can bring their humor, imaginations — and appetites.

Set up a snack station. A basket on the counter stocked with healthy snacks — fresh fruit, rice cakes, trail mix — makes a great invitation to wholesome eating. Or designate a shelf in the fridge for help-yourself nibbles, such as cheese sticks, yogurt, washed berries, celery sticks, and baby carrots.

Plan ahead. During the weekend, flip through these recipes with your child, pick out a few snacks for the week, then take him grocery shopping for any ingredients you don't already have. An hour of planning is a time-saver in disguise. With a well-stocked fridge and pantry, you'll successfully dodge those junky snacks during the rush of the school week.

CHAPTER ONE

Fun with Fruits and Veggies

WHEN IT COMES to getting healthy food into our kids, we're not beyond grating a zucchini into the brownie batter, or slipping a few shredded carrots under the pepperoni on their pizza. But here we offer you snacks that rely more on flamboyance than stealth: fruits and veggies moonlighting as flowers, reptiles, animals, and even the morning sun.

We can't promise that the Great Vegetable Wars at the dinner table will end, but our recipes are so playful and beautiful that they'll get your kids' attention. And these nourishing turn-ons boast more than fun preparation, good looks, and great nutrition — they're also delicious enough to keep your kids coming back for more. Our nutritious munchies taste so good, in fact, that your child may never guess that you're slipping in those five-a-day fruits and veggies.

Eat the rainbow. Teach your kids that eating a range of naturally colorful foods will give them all the vitamins they need to help keep them healthy. Split open a pomegranate and let them admire its ruby seeds, or show off the row of emerald green beads inside a pea pod. Remind your kids that nature puts on a colorful show to attract us to the healthy foods our bodies require.

Appetizer, anyone? Why wait until dinner to feed your kids their veggies? Try getting the goods into them when they're at their hungriest. While dinner cooks, put out baby carrots with salad dressing for dipping. Or let your kids make one of our fun and easy recipes, like Mr. Tomato Head (page 26) or Flying Fish (page 28). Consider these sneaky snacks vegetable side dishes made and eaten, and the veggie battle will be over before you even sit down to dinner.

Go on a produce expedition. Bring your kids grocery shopping and let them pick out one exotic or unusual-looking fruit or vegetable each week. How about a star fruit, a papaya, or a giant portobello mushroom? When you get home, let the kids prepare their new find as a snack. This adventurous tasting will foster broad and healthy eating habits.

Veg out with vegetables. If your kids tend to veg out in front of the television, try our Couch Potato Rule and make vegetables in any form (besides chips, of course!) the only snacks your kids are allowed to eat while watching the tube. You'll be amazed at how nutritious their favorite shows turn out to be.

Fresh Fruit Pizza, page 15

Strawberry Sparkles

It takes only a couple of minutes to turn a pint of fresh strawberries into a festive, mouthwatering treat.

Wash the berries and pat them dry with a paper towel. Fill a shallow bowl with colored sugar (you can buy this at the grocery store or mix your own by stirring two drops of food coloring into 1/4 cup of sugar).

In a mixing bowl, blend 4 ounces of softened cream cheese, 2 teaspoons of confectioners' sugar, 4 teaspoons of milk, and 1/2 teaspoon of vanilla extract with a fork until smooth and creamy. Add more milk, if necessary, to achieve the desired consistency.

Now, holding the berries by their stems, your kids can dip them into the cream cheese, roll them in the sugar, and enjoy.

Fruit Flowers

INVITE YOUR CHILD to plant these berry delicious flowers on his or her snack plate.

INGREDIENTS:
STRAWBERRY FLOWER:
- 3 strawberries
- 1 kiwi slice
-    Red shoestring licorice
- 2 mint leaves

RASPBERRY FLOWER:
- 10 raspberries
- 1 banana slice
-    Red shoestring licorice
- 2 mint leaves

DIRECTIONS:
Offer your child a selection of sliced fruits and help him or her create the flowers. For the flower centers, use a slice of banana or kiwi. Arrange raspberry or strawberry petals around it, then add a shoestring licorice stem with real mint leaves. Makes 2 flowers.

KIDS' STEPS: Kids can create and decorate their own fruit flowers.

Prep time: 5 minutes

Ladybugs on a Stick

A TRUE CROWD PLEASER, these luscious ladybugs are fun to bring into the classroom or to serve at a children's party.

INGREDIENTS:

4 red grapes
8 strawberries
40 mini chocolate chips
1 honeydew melon half
8 trimmed wooden skewers

DIRECTIONS:

For each ladybug, push half of a red grape onto a trimmed wooden skewer for the head. Next, push on a hulled strawberry body and score the back to create wings. For spots, use a toothpick to gently press mini chocolate chips, tips down, into the fruit. Arrange the skewers on a honeydew melon half. Makes 8 ladybugs.

KIDS' STEPS: Kids can spear the grapes and strawberries on the skewers.

Prep time: 20 minutes

PB & Apple

Jacob Meyer of Pomona, California, dubbed this simple innovation the "stuffed apple": a cored apple filled with peanut butter and topped with raisins. The filling keeps the apple from turning "brown and icky," says mom Rachel, who packs it in a plastic bag sealed with a twist tie.

Apple S'mores

SWEET-TASTING and good for you, apples make a great after-school snack. Here's a simple recipe for a treat from the Washington Apple Commission.

INGREDIENTS:

1   to 2 apples
    Lemon juice
½   cup peanut butter
2   tablespoons honey
½   teaspoon cinnamon
12 graham cracker squares

DIRECTIONS:

Core and cut the apples in half, then cut each half into 3 slices. Dip the apple wedges in lemon juice to prevent them from turning brown, then place them in a single layer on a microwave-safe plate.

Cover the apples with a paper towel and microwave on high for 1 to 2 minutes, or until they're tender but still hold their shape. (If your microwave does not have a carousel, rotate the dish halfway through cooking.)

Drain the apples on paper towels. In a small bowl, stir together the peanut butter, honey, and cinnamon. For each apple s'more, spread some of the peanut butter mixture on a graham cracker square, add 1 or 2 apple wedges, and top with a graham cracker lid. Makes 6 s'mores.

KIDS' STEPS: Kids can stir together the peanut butter and honey and assemble the apple s'mores.

Prep time: 10 minutes   Cooking time: 2 minutes

Easy Applesauce

NO MATTER how you slice them, apples are a favorite snack of kids. Here's how to turn your apples into sauce.

INGREDIENTS:

12	medium McIntosh apples
1	cup apple juice or water
½	cup sugar
½	tablespoon lemon juice
½	teaspoon cinnamon

DIRECTIONS:

Wash, peel, core, and thinly slice the apples, then place them in a large pot. Add the apple juice or water and bring to a boil. Reduce heat to medium-low, cover, and simmer until soft, about 15 minutes.

Remove from the stove and mash with a potato masher. Add sugar, lemon juice, and cinnamon and mix well. For a finer sauce, use a food mill. Cover and chill. Makes 4 to 5 cups.

PINK APPLESAUCE

This is as easy to make as its colorless counterpart. Just leave the skins on during cooking. Then, after adding the lemon juice, sugar, and cinnamon, press the apples through a food mill and let chill.

KIDS' STEPS: Kids can mash the cooked apples to make the sauce.

Snack Art

For a nutritious nibble and an after-school activity all in one, invite your kids to build edible art out of healthy foods. Simply scan your fridge and take out a selection of foods (limit the ingredients to 3 or 4 so you don't overwhelm your kids). Offer a tool, such as a plastic knife, a type of "cement" (see below), and a plate for a canvas. Then, invite youngsters to create faces, monsters, cars, flowers, or other delectable designs.

THE FOUNDATION:

Celery, carrot, or cucumber sticks or rounds; banana, apple, or pineapple slices; melon balls; lettuce leaves; or orange sections

THE CEMENT:

Peanut butter, cream cheese, cheese spread, yogurt, jam, or ranch dressing

THE DECORATIONS:

Seeds, nuts, grapes, raisins, olives, frozen peas (thawed), or beans

Prep time: 10 minutes   Cooking time: 20 minutes

Little Fruit-and-cheese Kebabs

HERE'S FURTHER evidence that everything has more kid appeal when stuck on a stick. These delightful kebabs can help satisfy a craving for sweets while providing such essentials as protein, vitamins, and fiber.

INGREDIENTS:

> Apple
> Cheddar cheese
> Raisins
> Toothpicks

DIRECTIONS:

Cut the apple and cheese into small cubes. Have a handful of raisins and a few toothpicks ready.

Let your kids make tiny apple, cheese, and raisin arrangements on the toothpicks in any order they like. (You can also use pineapple, strawberries, or pear.) Eat the kebabs soon after you make them, when they're still nice and fresh. Make as many as you'd like.

KIDS' STEPS: Kids can spear the apples pieces, cheese cubes, and raisins with toothpicks.

MY GREAT IDEA
Wiggle Worms

"After reading *The Very Hungry Caterpillar*, by Eric Carle, to my daughter, a preschooler at the time, she made a dozen edible caterpillars, ate half, and shared the rest with me.

"To make one, spear about four pieces of fruit onto a pretzel stick to make worms, leaving a tip at the end for the tail (parents can prespear the fruit). Join two worms with a piece of fruit for a longer creepy crawler. Use sprinkles to make tiny feet and mini chocolate chips to make eyes."

—*Penny Warner*
Danville, California

Prep time: 10 minutes

Strawberry-yogurt Smoothies and Pops

QUICK TRICK
Banana Scream

This banana shake makes a frosty treat. It's so thick, you'll want to serve it with a spoon instead of a straw.

Peel 3 bananas (the riper the banana, the sweeter the shake), cut them in half, wrap in plastic wrap, and freeze until firm. Place the frozen bananas in a blender, add 2 tablespoons of milk, and puree until blended and creamy like ice cream. Serve in small paper cups with small plastic spoons. Serves 4.

WHEN SCHOOL's out for the day, serve up a round of these fruity shakes. Customize your smoothies to suit your children's tastes (you can omit the banana, for example, and add blueberries in its place).

INGREDIENTS
- ½ pint fresh strawberries
- 1 banana
- 2 8-ounce containers nonfat strawberry yogurt
- 1 cup lowfat milk

DIRECTIONS:
Wash the strawberries, hull them, and pat them dry. Peel the banana and slice it in half or in quarters, then place all the fruit in an electric blender.

Spoon the yogurt into the blender, then pour in the milk. Cover, press the puree button, and blend until smooth and thoroughly combined, about 1 to 2 minutes.

Pour the shake into four 8-ounce glasses. For a creative presentation, garnish each drink with a fruit kebab (a strawberry and banana slice threaded on a bamboo skewer) and a colorful plastic straw. Makes 32 ounces, or four 8-ounce shakes.

STRAWBERRY SMOOTHIE POPS
Our Strawberry-yogurt Smoothie freezes into tasty pops that are fun to make and to eat. Carefully pour the smoothie mixture into a plastic pop mold. Freeze for 4 to 6 hours. Dip the mold in warm water, then unmold the pop. Makes 6 to 8 pops.

KIDS' STEPS: Kids can wash, hull, and pat dry the berries and pour the ingredients into the blender. If you're making pops, kids can pour the smoothie into the mold.

TIP: A Popsicle mold is a great investment for making healthy snacks like these Strawberry Smoothie Pops.

Prep time: 10 minutes

Fresh Fruit Pizza

SCHOOL MAY SATISFY a hunger for learning, but it also seems to inspire a ravenous appetite for junk food. A healthier alternative is the colorful fruit pizza shown on page 6, which chefs-in-training can cook up with a soupçon of adult supervision. Kids can munch on a slice or two after school and save the rest for after dinner.

INGREDIENTS:

1   ready-to-bake piecrust
        (or your favorite piecrust
        recipe)
½   cup soft-spread fat-free cream
        cheese
1   tablespoon sugar
¼   teaspoon vanilla extract
1   tablespoon milk
        A selection of berries and
        sliced fruits (blueberries,
        strawberries, bananas,
        kiwis, seedless grapes
        sliced in half, mandarin
        orange sections, and/or
        pineapple)
        Shredded coconut (optional)

DIRECTIONS:

Let the piecrust come to room temperature per the package instructions, then unfold it onto a large cookie sheet or pizza pan.

Roll up the edges of the crust, crimping them slightly so that they'll stay rolled. Prick the crust lightly with a fork in about 20 places (this will allow air to escape).

Bake the crust in a preheated 450° oven for about 9 minutes or until it's lightly browned. Remove from the oven and let it cool.

As the crust bakes, whisk together the cream cheese, sugar, and vanilla extract, adding the milk to make it spreadable.

When the crust has cooled, spread on the cream-cheese mixture with a rubber spatula, bringing it to the edge of the pizza.

Arrange the fruit on the pizza and don't stint on the creativity. Make a wild mosaic or a fruit face. If you like, sprinkle the pizza with shredded coconut. Slice with a sharp knife or pizza cutter and serve, or refrigerate. Serves 8.

KIDS' STEPS: Kids can mix up the cream cheese spread, arrange the fruit on the pizza, and sprinkle on the coconut.

DRINK UP

Raspberry Lime Rickey

Looking for a beverage that's refreshing and just sweet enough to please your kids' palates? Start with a generous scoop of raspberry sherbet in a tall frosted glass. Slowly pour in lime-flavored seltzer water until the froth reaches the top. Press another scoop of sherbet onto the glass rim and garnish with a slice of lime. Serve immediately with a straw and a spoon.

Prep time: 30 minutes   Cooking time: 9 minutes

Instant Sorbet

WHEN YOUR CHILD'S favorite fruit is in season, buy extra, cut it into chunks, and freeze it in sealed plastic bags. This way, you'll always have the makings of this delicious frozen snack.

INGREDIENTS:

- 2 cups 1-inch-cubes of fruit (try honeydew melon or papaya, or a combo, such as strawberry-watermelon or mango-cantaloupe)
- 2 to 4 tablespoons Simple Syrup (recipe follows)
- 1 to 2 tablespoons lemon or lime juice (optional)

DIRECTIONS:

Freeze the fruit in airtight plastic bags until solid (at least 6 hours). About 40 minutes before serving time, remove the fruit from the freezer and let it stand at room temperature.

Place the fruit in a food processor and pulse until it's finely chopped. Add Simple Syrup and lemon or lime juice to taste (the amount will depend on the ripeness of the fruit) and pulse until very creamy. Serve immediately. Makes 2 cups.

SIMPLE SYRUP

Place 1 cup of sugar in a bowl, add 1 cup of hot water, and stir to dissolve. Store in a jar in the refrigerator and use as needed.

KIDS' STEPS: Kids can cut up fruit with a plastic picnic knife and press the buttons on the food processor (with supervision, of course).

QUICK TRICK
Frozen Fruit Pops

Instead of reaching into the freezer for your average Popsicle, try one of these. Fruit pops are more fun because they have a unique shape, yummy taste, and no artificial flavors.

The best fruits to freeze: Banana halves, orange sections, whole strawberries without stems, mango spears, single grapes, and peeled kiwis.

How to make them: Slide the fruit on a Popsicle stick (use a toothpick for grapes), cover it with a plastic sandwich bag, secure it with a twist tie, and freeze for about 2 hours before serving. Tip: Freeze several pops per bag, unless the fruit is super-juicy (in which case the pops may stick together).

Prep time: 15 minutes   Freezing time: 6 hours
Thawing time: 40 minutes

Banana Bug

Now, here's a critter with real appeal. Have your kids poke pretzel sticks into a not-too-ripe banana for legs and antennae. Use peanut butter for eyes and to glue on the raisin spine. Now watch the kids devour the bug, one leg at a time.

Banana Pops

FROZEN BANANAS, chocolate, and crunchy toppings . . . what more could a kid ask for?

INGREDIENTS:

- 4 firm, ripe bananas
- 8 Popsicle sticks
- 1½ cups semisweet chocolate chips
- 2 tablespoons canola oil
  Toppings (shredded coconut and/or chopped nuts and sprinkles)
  Waxed paper–lined baking sheets

DIRECTIONS:

To make a bunch of these tempting treats, cut the bananas in half and insert a Popsicle stick halfway into each one. Set the pops on a waxed paper–lined baking sheet and place them in the freezer for 1 hour.

In a small saucepan over very low heat, stir together the chocolate chips and canola oil until melted. Place the toppings in individual bowls.

One at a time, remove the pops from the freezer and, holding them over the saucepan, spoon the chocolate over them. Roll each chocolate-covered banana in a topping, then return it to the freezer to harden for 1 to 2 hours before serving. Serves 8.

KIDS' STEPS: Kids can roll the chocolate-covered bananas in the toppings.

Prep time: 15 minutes   Freezing time: 2 to 3 hours

Arctic Oranges

A PRESCHOOL TEACHER came up with this clever and delicious idea. Her students added raisin eyes and an apple-wedge mouth.

INGREDIENTS:

- 4 oranges
- 4 cups orange juice
- 4 cherries
- Raisins (optional)
- Apple wedges (optional)

DIRECTIONS:

Cut the tops off the oranges in a zigzag pattern. Hollow out the insides, remove the seeds, and combine in the blender with the juice. Set the hollowed-out oranges in a muffin tin and fill them with the mixture. Drop a cherry inside each orange. Freeze for 2 to 3 hours. With toothpicks, attach raisin eyes and an apple wedge smile. Serve with a spoon and let the kids eat their way down to the surprise cherry. Serves 4.

KIDS' STEPS: Kids can press the buttons on the blender, carefully pour the juice into the oranges, and add the surprise cherry.

QUICK TRICK
Frozen Fruit Salad

Freeze the following fruit bites in a sealable bag for a fast and frosty treat: grapes, pineapple chunks, peach slices, apricot slices, banana slices, apple slices, cantaloupe balls, watermelon chunks, and orange wedges. Serve with plastic skewers or toothpicks.

Prep time: 15 minutes Freezing time: 2 to 3 hours

Fresh Fruit Ice

HELP YOUR KIDS WHIP up some fruit ice on a hot day, and set up a stand in your front yard. They'll sell out like nobody's business.

INGREDIENTS:

6 cups sliced strawberries or melon

½ cup partially thawed white grape-juice concentrate

½ cup water

DIRECTIONS:

Freeze the sliced fresh strawberries or melon until firm, but not solid, about 3 to 4 hours. Then blend the fruit with the partially thawed white grape-juice concentrate and the water in a blender or food processor. Spoon the mixture into serving cups. Serves 8 to 10.

KIDS' STEPS: Kids can blend the frozen fruit, juice, and water together and spoon the mixture into serving cups.

Prep time: 10 minutes Freezing time: 3 to 4 hours

Grapefruit Gal

THIS SOURPUSS is a clever way to slip vitamin C into your child's diet.

INGREDIENTS:
- 1 grapefruit
- Red or green grape clusters
- 2 red grapes
- 1 maraschino cherry, with stem
- Banana or apple slice (for mouth)

DIRECTIONS:
Cut a ¼-inch-thick slice out of the grapefruit and set it flat on a plate. Arrange the red or green grape clusters around the top of the grapefruit for hair.

Add red grape eyes, a maraschino cherry nose, and a big grin made of an apple or banana slice. Serves 1.

KIDS' STEPS: Kids can arrange the fruity features on the grapefruit slice.

MY GREAT IDEA
Kid Coolers

"For summertime fun, and to keep the kids from running in and out of the kitchen all day, I fill plastic soda bottles with fruit juice, Kool-Aid, or lemonade and freeze them (I leave room at the top because water expands when it freezes). Then, when the kids are off to the playground or pool, I can hand them frozen drinks that stay cool for hours."

— *Dot Price*
Montgomery, Alabama

Prep time: 10 minutes

Mix-your-own Maple-vanilla Yogurt

YOGURT THAT COMES already flavored is fun to eat, but it's often full of sugar. Parents will appreciate how good this mix-your-own kind tastes with just a moderate amount of sweetening. And even toddlers can accomplish this simple cooking project.

INGREDIENTS:

1½ cups plain yogurt
¼ cup real maple syrup
½ teaspoon vanilla extract
Strawberry jam (optional)
Mint leaves (optional)

DIRECTIONS:

Measure the yogurt into a medium-size bowl. Add the maple syrup and vanilla extract and mix until they disappear into the yogurt.

Spoon into small bowls. Let your kids decorate each serving with dabs of strawberry jam and a tiny mint leaf, if desired. Serves 4.

KIDS' STEPS: Kids can stir in and mix the maple syrup and vanilla extract, then decorate each serving.

QUICK TRICK
Party Parfait

A creative presentation makes an ordinary snack, like yogurt and fresh fruit, seem extraordinary. If you don't have parfait glasses, find other fancy glasses, preferably transparent ones so the kids can see the layers.

Fill a parfait glass halfway with plain or vanilla yogurt. Add a layer of fresh fruit and granola or another favorite cereal. Spoon in more yogurt and add another layer of fruit and granola or cereal. Refrigerate until serving time.

Prep time: 5 minutes

Rancher's Delight

Once your kids have stirred up our ranch dressing at right, they can arrange fresh crudités into a down-home design on a platter. Form the outline of a cowboy boot using green pepper slices, then fill in with rows of mini carrots, cherry tomatoes, cucumber slices, celery, mushrooms, and cauliflower. As a finishing touch, add a bell pepper toe and spur. Serve with the ranch dip.

LET YOUR KIDS play with their food — and make this creative crudité. Once their flower is in bloom, they can dip the petals in our easy-to-mix ranch dressing.

INGREDIENTS:

FLOWER:

Assorted vegetables, such as radish slices, fresh spinach leaves, cucumber rounds, cherry tomatoes, celery sticks, and baby carrots

RANCH DIP:

¼ cup mayonnaise
¾ cup buttermilk
2 teaspoons cider vinegar
¼ teaspoon salt
1 teaspoon onion powder
½ teaspoon garlic powder

DIRECTIONS:

FLOWER:

Set out assorted vegetables and let your kids design their own flowers (there is no right or wrong way of doing this). Here, we used radish slices and cucumber rounds for petals, cherry tomatoes for flower centers, celery sticks for stems, spinach for leaves, and baby carrots for grass.

RANCH DIP:

To make the ranch dip, place all the ingredients in a medium-size bowl. Mix well with a whisk. Eat right away with the vegetable flowers, or refrigerate in a covered container until you're ready to use it. Makes 1 cup.

KIDS' STEPS: Kids can design the veggie flowers and help you measure and mix up the ranch dip.

Prep time: 20 minutes

Mr. Tomato Head

Bright and cheerful, these pea-brained fellows may actually tempt your child to eat vegetables. With a serrated knife (parents only), slice the top off a small tomato or cherry tomato; reserve the top for the hat. Scoop out the inside with a teaspoon or melon baller, turn the tomato upside down to drain, then fill with peas. Your child can use cream cheese to glue on a pair of canned black-bean eyes, a yellow pepper nose, and a celery grin. Put his hat back on, and he's ready to paint the town red.

Cherry Tomato and Cucumber Bites

KIDS LOVE squirting this basil cream cheese through a pastry bag and into hollowed-out cherry tomatoes and cucumber slices. Use room-temperature cream cheese for best results.

INGREDIENTS:

- 1 8-ounce package cream cheese, softened
- ¼ cup finely chopped basil leaves
- 1 garlic clove, crushed
- 1 tablespoon grated Parmesan cheese (optional)

  Cucumbers and cherry tomatoes

  Fresh dill (optional)

DIRECTIONS:

In a small mixing bowl, stir the cream cheese until smooth. Add the chopped basil, garlic, and Parmesan, if desired, and stir until thoroughly combined. Set aside.

Score the sides of a cucumber, if desired, with a zester, potato peeler, or knife. Next, cut the cucumber into 1-inch-thick rounds and carefully scoop out the seeds with a melon baller. Slice off the tops of the cherry tomatoes with a serrated knife and scoop out the insides with the baller.

Fill a pastry bag, fitted with a star tip, with the cream cheese. If you don't have a pastry bag, fill a sealable freezer bag with cream cheese and snip off a small hole in the corner.

Squirt the cream cheese through the bag into the hollowed-out cucumbers and tomatoes. Garnish with sprigs of fresh dill, if desired, and serve immediately. Makes 1 cup of flavored cream cheese, enough to fill 30 vegetables.

KIDS' STEPS: Kids can use a melon baller to hollow out the veggies and a pastry bag to fill them with flavored cream cheese.

Prep time: 20 minutes

Peanut-ginger Dipping Sauce

FOR A QUICK appetizer or light supper, serve this warm dipping sauce with leftover chicken and fresh vegetables.

INGREDIENTS:
- ½ cup peanut butter
- ¾ to 1 cup water
- 1 tablespoon soy sauce
  Fresh gingerroot
- 1 cup cubed cooked chicken
  Baby carrots and snow peas
- 1 scallion, chopped (optional)

DIRECTIONS:
In a small saucepan, whisk the peanut butter and water until smooth. Stir in the soy sauce.

Peel the ginger with a potato peeler or knife. Grate the gingerroot until you have 1 packed teaspoon. Stir it into the peanut mixture.

Transfer the saucepan to a stove top and heat on medium-low. Cook the sauce for about 3 to 5 minutes, stirring occasionally. Add extra water to thin the sauce, if necessary.

Meanwhile, spear each piece of the cubed chicken with a toothpick. Set the pieces on a platter along with the fresh snow peas and baby carrots.

Pour the warm peanut sauce into a small bowl and garnish with chopped scallions, if desired. Have the kids dip the chicken and veggies into the sauce. Serves 4 to 6.

KIDS' STEPS: Older kids can grate the fresh ginger and cook the sauce on the stove top (with supervision). Younger kids can spear the chicken cubes with toothpicks and arrange the foods on the platter.

MY GREAT IDEA
Self-Serve Salad Bar

"Getting my two-and-a-half-year-old son, Jack, to eat vegetables was a hassle until I started serving him a 'salad bar' of his own. I fill the six cups of a small muffin tin with grated cheese, peas, croutons, chopped hard-boiled eggs, carrots, and lettuce. Then I give him a bowl and a tiny pitcher of salad dressing. Jack has a blast making his own salad, and he eats the whole thing."

— *Kate Romero*

Via e-mail

Prep time: 15 minutes Cooking time: 5 minutes

Flying Fish

Turn a handful of fresh snow peas into a school of fanciful fish.

Begin with a snow pea body, then add triangular fins cut from a yellow pepper (use a clean pair of scissors or paring knife). For a tail, cut a second pea pod into a V. Have your kids give their finny friend a sliced green olive eye, glued in place with cream cheese. Who wouldn't take the bait?

Green Bean Serpents

MONSTERS FOR SNACK? Don't worry, all these serpents will scare up is a healthy appetite.

INGREDIENTS:
Fresh green beans
Dry-roasted sunflower seeds
Mustard or cream cheese

DIRECTIONS:
Poke dry-roasted sunflower seeds into the back of a fresh green bean. If the seeds fall out, keep them in place with dabs of mustard or cream cheese. You can also add eyes with tiny squirts of mustard.

KIDS' STEPS: Kids can poke the sunflowers in the beans.

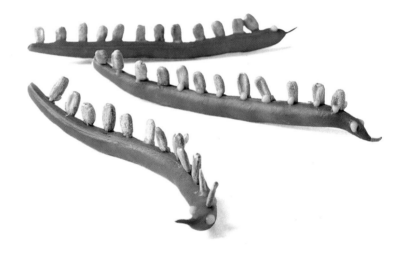

Prep time: 10 minutes

World's Easiest Pickles

ALL YOU NEED to make this peck of pickles is your refrigerator and a few common ingredients.

INGREDIENTS:

- 4 medium cucumbers
- 1 teaspoon salt
- 2 cups sugar
- 1 cup diced, red onion
- 1 cup chopped green bell pepper
- 1 cup cider vinegar
- 1 teaspoon celery seed
- 1 teaspoon dill weed (optional)

DIRECTIONS:

Wash the cucumbers thoroughly and cut them into spears. Mix the cucumbers and salt in a medium-size bowl and let them sit at room temperature for 1 hour.

Next, stir in the sugar, onion, green pepper, vinegar, celery seed, and, if desired, dill. Cover the bowl, refrigerate overnight, and your pickles are done. Keep refrigerated and the pickles should last several weeks. Makes 32 to 48 pickles.

KIDS' STEPS: Kids can measure and mix the pickling ingredients.

QUICK TRICK
Yellow Pepper Sun

Your child can brighten up his or her snack plate with this vegetable sun. Cut a yellow bell pepper in half and remove the inner ribs and seeds. Cut a 1-inch circle for the sun (or substitute a carrot round) and add six pepper-strip rays.

**Prep time: 15 minutes Marinating time: 1 hour
Chilling time: 12 hours**

CHAPTER TWO

Chips and Munchies

WHETHER YOUR family's curling up to watch a video, camping in the backyard, or simply struck by the urge for one of those irresistible, addictive crunchies, look no further. Our roster of savory treats offers all of the munchable satisfaction that kids crave, with the added benefit that you'll actually know — and be able to pronounce — the ingredients that go into them.

Our healthier versions of kid-favorite snack foods, like Tortilla Chip Strips (page 37), Easy Cheesy Crackers (page 33), and soft pretzels (page 32), are appealing, inexpensive, and fun to make. And your child's creative involvement in the process might mean healthier portions, too: instead of sitting down with an open bag of chips, she'll be busy crafting her own wholesome treat. But don't take it from us — let your kids try these recipes for themselves. They're the experts, after all.

Wrap it up. Half the fun of store-bought snacks is the bells-and-whistles packaging. Stay competitive by packing up your homemade varieties in inviting containers. Try tiny, sealable plastic bags, brightly colored disposable containers, and pastel plastic wrap — any of which will jazz up even the simplest edible take-alongs.

Dip it good. Never underestimate the interactive pleasure of dipping. Many finicky eaters live by the philosophy, "If I can dip it, I'll try it!" In this chapter we offer dips, such as Farmstand Salsa (page 39) and Healthy Hummus Dip (page 38). Now all you'll need are the dippers, from chips and bread sticks to baby carrots and green pepper slices.

Keep your cool. Your typical cracker or chip snacks can take some heat, but every now and then you might want to pack cheese, yogurt, or salsa. How do you keep them cool in your child's backpack? Putting them in an insulated snack bag with a reusable ice pack is one solution, but you can also pack them with a frozen, partially full water bottle (water expands when it freezes) or a frozen juice box. Each acts like an ice pack but becomes a cold and slushy drink later in the day. Frozen portable yogurt tubes also make deliciously edible ice packs.

Take a hike. Pack up any of our baggable munchies — try the Feeling Nutty Oat Bars (page 41) or the Popcorn-Banana Munch Mix (page 43) — and hit the great outdoors. Walking is good exercise, and a fun, wholesome treat to crunch along the way can provide just the incentive your kids need to get their bodies moving.

Healthy Hummus Dip

QUICK TRICK
Easy Pita Chips

These healthful chips are easy for kids to make and, some say, even tastier than baked tortilla chips.

Heat the oven to 375°. Cut a sandwich-size pita into sixths. Pull apart the top and bottom of each wedge. Lay the wedges on a baking sheet, brush with olive oil, if you like, and bake until crisp and slightly brown, about 5 minutes. Serves 2.

IT'S NO WONDER that this cholesterol-free, sugar-free spread is popular in Middle Eastern countries — it's good for you and delicious with crackers, raw veggies, or the Easy Pita Chips at left. After you realize how easy it is to make, your family is likely to form its own healthy hummus habit.

INGREDIENTS:

- 1 15-ounce can garbanzo beans, drained and rinsed
- 2 garlic cloves, chopped
- ¼ cup cold water
- 1 teaspoon salt
- 5 tablespoons lemon juice
- ⅓ cup tahini paste

DIRECTIONS:
Mix all of the ingredients in a food processor and pulse until smooth, scraping the sides often with a spatula.

If you don't own a food processor, you can mix the hummus by hand. Use a potato masher to mash the beans, garlic, water, and salt until smooth. Then use a spoon to beat in the lemon juice, then the tahini. Makes 1½ cups.

KIDS' STEPS: Kids can measure ingredients and press the buttons on the food processor or mash the ingredients with a potato masher.

Prep time: 15 minutes

Farm-stand Salsa

KNOWN ALSO as *pico de gallo* or *salsa fresca*, this is one of the simplest salsas to make. And it tastes great scooped up on your favorite tortilla chips or nachos.

INGREDIENTS:

- 2 large ripe tomatoes
- 4 scallions
- 1 mild green chili or 1 small green bell pepper
- ¼ to ½ cup lightly packed cilantro leaves or Italian parsley leaves
- ½ lemon or lime
  Salt to taste

DIRECTIONS:

Core the tomatoes, and cut them crosswise into ¼-inch-thick slices. Finely dice the slices and transfer them to a medium-size bowl.

Wash the scallions well, then trim off the trailing strands of the root end, as well as any sections that don't look or feel crisp. Slice thinly, then mix with the tomatoes.

Slice open the chili or green pepper and scrape away any seeds. Dice the chili or pepper and add it to the tomatoes. (Note: If using a chili, wash your hands well afterward, as the chili's oil can irritate your skin.) Finely chop the cilantro or parsley leaves and stir them into the salsa.

Squeeze the juice from the lemon or lime half and pour it into the salsa. Stir the mixture. Add a generous pinch of salt and stir again. Cover and chill it for 30 minutes.

Just before serving, sample a spoonful and add more citrus juice and salt if desired. Makes about 2 cups.

KIDS' STEPS: Kids can help dice the tomato slices with a plastic knife, squeeze the lemon or lime to make juice, and stir the salsa.

QUICK TRICK
Creamy Guacamole

The main ingredient in this traditional Mexican dip is a fruit (yep, avocado's a fruit) so tasty that kids will never guess it's also packed with vitamins and minerals. In fact, one cup of avocado has more potassium than an equal serving of bananas.

- 2 ripe avocados
- 2 tablespoons sour cream
- 3 tablespoons bottled or Farm-stand Salsa, at left
- 1 teaspoon lemon juice
- ¼ teaspoon salt
  Black pepper to taste

Cut the avocados in half, remove the pits, and spoon the flesh out of the skins and into a medium-size bowl. Mash the avocados with a fork, then add the sour cream, salsa, lemon juice, and salt and mix well. Season with black pepper and serve immediately. Delicious with Tortilla Chip Strips (page 37) and Veggie Quesadillas (page 67). Makes 1½ cups.

Prep time: 20 minutes Chilling time: 30 minutes

Cookies-and-milk Bars

COOKIE-BASED SNACK bars are often laden with sugar. This homemade version uses chocolate graham crackers — less sweet, but still kid pleasing — and sneaks in low-fat granola and nuts for a more wholesome snack. You can also add dried fruit bits or wheat germ for extra nutrition.

INGREDIENTS:

- 8 chocolate graham crackers (or 10 reduced-fat chocolate sandwich cookies), broken into chunks
- 1 cup low-fat granola (or toasted oat-based cereal)
- ⅓ cup white chocolate chips
- ½ cup walnut or pecan pieces, coarsely chopped
- ½ cup fat-free or low-fat sweetened condensed milk

DIRECTIONS:

Heat the oven to 350°. Coat an 8-by 8-inch baking pan with cooking spray. In a medium-size bowl, combine the graham crackers, granola, white chocolate chips, and walnuts or pecans and mix well. Drizzle the condensed milk over the top and stir until well blended.

Using a piece of waxed paper, press the mixture firmly into the prepared pan. Bake for 20 to 25 minutes, or until just golden and set. Cool completely. Cut into bars. Makes 10.

KIDS' STEPS: Kids can break up the graham crackers, mix the ingredients, and press the mixture into the pan.

Prep time: 15 minutes Baking time: 25 minutes

Feeling Nutty Oat Bars

THESE NO-BAKE bars combine the chewy crunch of puffed rice with the heartiness of peanut butter. And they take just minutes to make.

INGREDIENTS:

- 1 tablespoon butter or margarine
- ⅓ cup creamy peanut butter
- 2 cups miniature marshmallows, lightly packed
- 1 cup low-fat granola
- 1 cup puffed rice cereal
- ⅓ cup coarsely chopped cocktail peanuts

DIRECTIONS:

Coat an 8- by 8-inch baking pan with cooking spray. Put the butter or margarine, peanut butter, and marshmallows into a medium-size microwave-safe bowl and microwave on high for 30 seconds, or until the mixture is just melted. Stir to blend.

Microwave again briefly if the mixture isn't melted and smooth. Stir in the granola, puffed rice, and peanuts (or mix it with greased bare hands — make sure it's not too hot). Spread the mixture in the prepared pan, flattening it evenly with a sheet of waxed paper. Let it cool, then cut it into bars. Makes 8 bars.

KIDS' STEPS: Kids can stir the granola, puffed rice, and peanuts into the melted mixture and help spread the nutty oats in the pan.

QUICK TRICK
Cereal Solution

Here's the perfect snack mix recipe for those times when you've got several kinds of cereal in the cupboard but not a full serving in any one box.

In a large bowl, combine 3 cups of assorted cereals with ⅓ cup *each* of raisins, peanuts, and pretzels.

Melt 4 ounces of white chocolate in the top of a double boiler. Alternatively, place the chips in a shallow microwave-safe bowl, microwave on high for 1 minute, stir, and microwave for 30 seconds more. Stir the melted chips into the cereal mixture until the bits are well coated. Chill for 20 to 30 minutes, then serve. Makes 4 cups.

Prep time: 10 minutes Cooking time: 1 minute

Popcorn-Banana Munch Mix

KIDS HAVE a great time concocting this creative snack mix. Simply start with cheesy popcorn, then mix in some of your favorite healthy snack foods — banana chips, peanuts, and dried cranberries — to create a flavor surprise.

INGREDIENTS:

> 6 cups Cheddar popcorn
> 1 to 2 cups banana chips,
>   broken into small pieces
> 2 cups dry-roasted peanuts
> 1 to 2 cups sweetened, dried
>   cranberries

DIRECTIONS:
Measure all the ingredients into a big bowl (you can substitute your family's favorite natural snack foods, if desired).

Stir well, then dig in. Makes 9 to 11 cups.

KIDS' STEPS: Kids can measure and mix up the munch mix.

Prep time: 5 minutes

COOKING TIP
Flavored Popcorn

Leave a bowl of fresh popcorn on the counter for when your kids come home from school — serve it as is or spice it up. To 4 cups of popped popcorn, add these flavorings:

CHEESE POPCORN

Mix $1/4$ cup grated Parmesan cheese with $1^1/2$ tablespoons melted butter or margarine and toss with popcorn.

TEX-MEX POPCORN

Add $1/8$ teaspoon chili powder or $1/4$ teaspoon taco seasoning to melted butter, pour over popcorn, and toss.

PIZZA POPCORN

Mix $1/4$ teaspoon each of oregano, basil, and parsley into melted butter before tossing.

SWEET CINNAMON POPCORN

Shake popcorn with cinnamon sugar.

Cupboard Snack Mix

QUICK TRICK
Fishes in a Pond

Here's a fun variation on the classic celery, peanut butter, and raisin snack known as Ants on a Log. Here, we've made Fishes in a Pond. But you could also create Ducks in the Lake, using "quackers" (crackers) dipped in melted cheese.

Scoop ½ cup low-fat cream cheese or cheese spread into a bowl (you can tint the cream cheese with blue coloring to make it look like water). Place fish-shaped crackers in a separate bowl. Let the kids dip celery sticks into the cheese, then into the bowl of crackers to "catch" a fish. Serves 2.

BITE-SIZE CEREAL, dried fruit, pretzels, nuts, crackers, shredded coconut — anything goes when you're tossing together a homemade snack mix, says *FamilyFun* reader Lori Murray of Columbus, Ohio. Lori also throws in M&M's or chocolate chips "if I'm in a good mood," she says, and mixes it all up in a plastic bag. Daughter Caitlin, twelve, enjoys coming up with her own concoctions, while son Billy, seven, likes the shaking the best.

INGREDIENTS:
- 4 cup pretzel twists
- 1 cup cheddar Goldfish crackers
- 1 cup Chex cereal
- 1 cup banana chips
- ¼ cup M&M's
- ¼ cup raisins
- ¼ cup mixed nuts

DIRECTIONS:
Place all the ingredients in a gallon-size sealable plastic bag, seal, and shake until well mixed. Makes about 4½ cups.

KIDS' STEPS: Kids can measure and mix up the snack mix ingredients.

Prep time: 10 minutes

Microwave Nut Crunch

ANY COMBINATION OF nuts can be used for this recipe, but we like including pecans and almonds because they contain impressive amounts of heart-healthy monounsaturated fats.

INGREDIENTS:

- 1 cup pecan halves
- 1 cup whole almonds
- ½ cup walnut halves
- ½ cup sugar
- 1 teaspoon ground cinnamon
- ⅛ teaspoon salt
- 3 tablespoons whole milk
- 1 teaspoon vanilla extract

DIRECTIONS:
Heat the oven to 350° and spread the nuts in a single layer on a baking sheet. Roast them for about 8 to 10 minutes, or until they just start to turn brown.

Stir together the sugar, cinnamon, salt, and milk in a large microwave-safe mixing bowl. Microwave on high for 2 minutes. Stir quickly (don't worry if the mixture looks as though it curdled a little), then microwave for 1 minute more, or until the mixture is noticeably thick. Stir in the vanilla extract, then stir in the nuts, turning them to coat.

Spoon the nuts onto waxed paper, separate them with a fork, and let them cool for 10 minutes. Place ¼-cup servings in little plastic containers or sealable plastic bags for individual snack packs. Makes 10 servings.

KIDS' STEPS: Kids can measure ingredients, press the buttons on the microwave, and spoon the nuts onto waxed paper.

Prep time: 10 minutes Cooking time: 13 minutes

CHAPTER THREE

Finger Foods

KIDS KNOW that just about anything eaten without utensils tastes better — and our dozens of finger foods are just the right size for little hands. Bigger than a small snack, but smaller than a big meal, these are the munchies to turn to when your kids are starving, without a meal in sight.

And don't worry if they fill up — these little bites offer big helpings of energy. They're substantial enough, in fact, to pinch-hit for a real meal, thanks to their wholesome (and appealing) ingredients. The colorful veggie add-ons, for instance, add character as well as nutrition to recipes like the Bagel Critters (page 57) or Deviled R-egg-atta (page 55). And because of the recipes' quick preparation, easy tricks (think: cookie cutters), and kid-pleasing names, such as Pizza Muffins (page 49) and Butterfly Cheese-wich (page 58), kids will be eager to make as well as eat their creations.

Let them graze. Little meals are in — at least that's what the trendy restaurants tell us. But our kids have known this all along, often preferring teeny-tiny appetizers over a full plate of food. We're not recommending that you give up on regular meals, but go ahead and indulge this grazing habit occasionally by serving a plate of finger foods for lunch or dinner: veggie-filled Spiral Sandwiches (page 60) or Peanutty

Drumsticks (page 65). Dress them up with toothpicks and paper doilies, and your mini meal will feel like a party.

Think inside the box — the lunch box, that is. Many of the recipes in this chapter make super school lunches. They're quickly assembled and portable, and children are delighted to eat a sub sandwich they've assembled themselves (page 64) or a cheerful Pita Rabbit (page 62) instead of the predictable PB&J.

Make your own snack packs. Packaged snack meals — which let kids construct cracker sandwiches and other treats — have great kid appeal, but they can be costly. The alternative: home-made "mom-ables." Cut cheese and meat slices into squares or circles with a cookie cutter and pack them with the cracker of your choice. Or pack a small Boboli pizza round with a small container of pizza sauce, shredded mozzarella cheese, and sliced pepperoni for eating away from home.

Stay alert to allergies. With sensitivities, especially to peanuts, on the rise, it's more important than ever to find out if your child's playmates have any food allergies. Because it's a protein-rich kid pleaser, we use peanut butter in a number of our finger foods. But we also offer a slew of savory nibbles and sandwiches for nutless snacking — try the Lunch Guests (page 63) and Bob and Betty Bread (page 59).

Pizza Muffins

THESE LITTLE CORN muffins have the pizza flavor kids crave in a handy bite-size package. Eat them warm, right from the paper liners.

INGREDIENTS:

MUFFIN BATTER:

1½ cups all-purpose flour
½ cup fine yellow cornmeal
1 tablespoon sugar
2 teaspoons baking powder
½ teaspoon salt
1 large egg, lightly beaten
1¼ cups milk
¼ cup vegetable oil

TOPPING:

⅓ cup marinara sauce
⅓ cup grated Parmesan cheese
⅓ cup finely chopped pepperoni

DIRECTIONS:

Heat the oven to 400° and line about 36 mini muffin cups with paper liners.

Sift the flour, cornmeal, sugar, baking powder, and salt into a large mixing bowl. In a separate bowl, blend the egg, milk, and vegetable oil. Make a well in the dry mixture and add the liquid. Stir the batter until combined.

In a small bowl, blend the marinara sauce and Parmesan cheese; set aside.

Spoon the batter into the muffin-pan liners, filling them about three-quarters full. Spoon about ½ teaspoon of the sauce-and-cheese mixture on top of each one, pushing it in slightly, then sprinkle with chopped pepperoni.

Bake the muffins for 15 minutes; they'll puff up and brown slightly around the upper edge. Cool in the pan for several minutes, then remove from the pan and eat warm. Makes about 36 mini muffins.

KIDS' STEPS: Kids can measure and mix the ingredients, spoon the batter into the muffin cups, and sprinkle on the pepperoni bits.

QUICK TRICK
Instant Pizzas

Got a minute? Try one of these fine freestyle pizzas. Bake them in your regular oven or toaster oven.

THE MEX MELT

Heat a flour tortilla in the oven. Spread with guacamole (see page 39), top with sliced olives, chopped tomato, and Monterey Jack or Cheddar cheese. Broil until cheese melts.

THE FRENCH BREAD CLASSIC

Halve loaves lengthwise. Toast lightly in the oven. Spread with marinara sauce, top with grated or shredded cheese and sliced pepperoni. Bake in the oven until the cheese melts.

STUFFED PITA PIZZA

Halve pitas crosswise, stuff with The French Bread Classic ingredients (above). Brush with olive oil. Pan-cook the pitas like grilled cheese.

ENGLISH MUFFIN PIZZA

Toast halves lightly. Spread with marinara sauce, top with sliced pepperoni, diced green peppers, and/or sliced olives. Sprinkle on grated mozzarella. Broil until the cheese melts.

Prep time: 20 minutes   Cooking time: 15 minutes

Easy Applesauce Muffins

THESE CINNAMON-LACED muffins are made with chunky applesauce instead of sliced apples. Enjoy them on a crisp fall afternoon, or pack them into lunch boxes.

INGREDIENTS:

- 6 tablespoons butter
- 1½ cups all-purpose flour
- 1 teaspoon baking powder
- ½ teaspoon baking soda
- 1 teaspoon cinnamon
- ½ teaspoon salt
- 2 eggs
- ⅔ cup brown sugar
- 1½ cups chunky applesauce

DIRECTIONS:

Heat the oven to 375° and line a 12-cup muffin tin with paper liners. In a small microwave-safe bowl, melt the butter in the microwave on high for about 30 to 60 seconds; set aside to cool slightly.

Sift together the flour, baking powder, baking soda, cinnamon, and salt into a large mixing bowl.

In another large bowl, whisk together the eggs and brown sugar. Stir in the applesauce and melted butter until the mixture is smooth.

Pour the apple mixture over the flour mixture. Mix with a wooden spoon until combined.

Fill the bake cups about two-thirds full with batter. Bake for 20 minutes, or until light brown. Test for doneness by inserting a knife in the middle of one muffin. If it comes out clean, the muffins are ready to eat. Makes 12.

KIDS' STEPS: Kids can measure and mix the ingredients and spoon the batter into muffin cups.

Prep time: 20 minutes   Baking time: 20 minutes

Banana Chocolate-chip Mini Muffins

DON'T BE FOOLED by their diminutive size. These morsels are packed with two big flavors, and their bite-size scale means you can have seconds, thirds, even fourths!

INGREDIENTS:

- 1½ cups all-purpose flour
- ⅔ cup sugar
- 1½ teaspoons baking powder
- ¼ teaspoon salt
- 1 cup mashed, very ripe bananas (about 2 large or 3 medium)
- 1 large egg
- ¼ cup (½ stick) butter, melted
- ¼ cup fat-free or light sour cream
- 2 teaspoons vanilla extract
- ½ cup mini semisweet chocolate chips
- ¼ cup low-fat milk

DIRECTIONS:

Heat the oven to 350°. Line about 36 mini muffin cups with paper liners, or lightly coat the cups with cooking spray.

Combine the flour, sugar, baking powder, and salt in a medium-size bowl and stir with a fork to blend.

In a mixing bowl, combine the mashed bananas, egg, melted butter, sour cream, milk, and vanilla extract. Beat on medium until well blended. Reduce the speed to low and blend in the dry ingredients (do not overmix). Stir in the mini chocolate chips.

Fill each muffin cup with 1 level tablespoon of batter. Bake the muffins for about 20 minutes, or until the tops are golden and a tooth-pick comes out with some melted chocolate but no crumbs. Transfer the muffins to a rack to cool. Makes 36 mini muffins.

KIDS' STEPS: Kids can mash the bananas, measure and mix the ingredients, and spoon batter into muffin tins.

Prep time: 15 minutes   Baking time: 20 minutes

Treats on a Stick

When glowing coals beckon her family on camping trips, *FamilyFun* reader Debbie Fohr of Collinsville, Illinois, makes Dough Boys: cold biscuit dough stretched and coiled around thick peeled sticks, then roasted over the fire.

Another reader, Kerri De Ruiter of Crestwood, Illinois, bakes her biscuits the same way, then rolls them in butter and cinnamon sugar. Her three kids gobble up these campy "cinnamon rolls."

Homemade Biscuit Mix

KEEP A BATCH of this mix in your fridge, and your kids can roll up their very own biscuits for a snack — or for tonight's dinner.

INGREDIENTS:

MIX:

- 3 cups all-purpose flour
- 1½ cups whole-wheat flour
- 1 teaspoon salt
- 2 tablespoons baking powder
- 1 cup cold butter, cut into pieces

BISCUITS:

- 2 cups of Homemade Biscuit Mix
- ⅓ to ⅔ cup buttermilk or milk
  Poppy or sesame seeds, Parmesan cheese, or dried herbs in shakers (optional)

DIRECTIONS:

MIX:

In a large bowl, mix together the all-purpose and whole-wheat flour, salt, and baking powder. Then use a pastry cutter or fork to blend in the butter until it has the consistency of cornmeal. Scoop into a large jar or a gallon-size sealable plastic bag and store in the refrigerator for up to two weeks.

BISCUITS:

Heat the oven to 425°. In a medium-size bowl, stir together the biscuit mix with the buttermilk or milk until a soft dough forms. Turn the dough onto a floured surface, knead a few times, and then roll it out to about a ½-inch thickness. Use 2-inch cookie cutters to make the biscuits.

Place the biscuits on an ungreased baking sheet, and sprinkle with poppy or sesame seeds, Parmesan cheese, or dried herbs for decorations, if desired. Bake the biscuits for 10 to 12 minutes, or until lightly browned. Makes ten 2-inch biscuits.

KIDS' STEPS: Kids can measure and mix up the ingredients, knead the dough, and cut out the biscuits with cookie cutters.

Prep time: 20 minutes   Baking time: 12 minutes

Pigs in a Blanket

EATEN PLAIN OR dipped in mustard, these cute little biscuit sandwiches have a mini smoked sausage rolled up inside. Like any biscuits, the fresher these are, the better, so prepare them as close to snack time as possible.

INGREDIENTS:

- 2 cups all-purpose flour
- 1 tablespoon sugar
- 2 teaspoons baking powder
- ½ teaspoon baking soda
- ½ teaspoon salt
- 4 tablespoons cold unsalted butter, cut into ¼-inch pieces
- ½ cup grated Cheddar cheese
- ¾ cup buttermilk
- 18 mini smoked sausages

DIRECTIONS:

Heat the oven to 400˚. Lightly grease a large baking sheet. Sift the flour, sugar, baking powder, baking soda, and salt into a mixing bowl.

Scatter the butter pieces over the dry ingredients and rub them into the flour until the mixture becomes crumbly. Stir in the cheese so that it's evenly distributed.

Make a well in the dry mixture and pour the buttermilk into it. Stir well with a wooden spoon. Let the dough sit for 3 minutes.

Sprinkle some extra flour over the dough, then stir it once or twice again and turn it out onto a well-floured surface. With floured hands, pat the dough into a 15- by 7-inch rectangle, handling it as little as possible so the biscuits will be tender.

Slice the rectangle into thirds, first horizontally, then vertically. Next, slice each of the resulting 9 smaller rectangles diagonally to create 18 narrow triangles. (Note: Slicing the triangles is a snap if you use a pizza cutter. For the best results, trim the sides of the rectangle so that it's symmetrical before making the other cuts.)

One at a time, roll up the sausages in the dough triangles. Place the wrapped sausages pointy end down on the greased baking sheet.

Bake the crescents for 12 to 13 minutes, until golden brown. Cool them on the sheet for 3 minutes, then transfer them to a wire cooling rack. Makes 18.

KIDS' STEPS: Kids can sift the dry ingredients, rub in the butter, shape the dough, and roll up the sausages.

TIP: To wrap each sausage, brush any excess flour from the biscuit triangle. Then, starting at the triangle base, lightly pinch the dough against the sausage link and roll it toward the tip.

QUICK TRICK
Freckle-face Bears

Planning a teddy bear tea party? Serve up these adorable cubs.

- 1 10-ounce package refrigerator biscuits
- ¼ cup sesame or sunflower seeds
- 36 raisins

Heat the oven to 400° and spray a cookie sheet with nonstick cooking spray. Roll six biscuits into balls, roll the balls in the seeds, then flatten each one slightly on the cookie sheet to form a bear's head. Use small pieces of dough for ears and noses and raisins for eyes. (Use the leftover dough to create letters, monsters, faces, or pigs.) Bake for 8 to 10 minutes. Makes 6 bears.

Hard-boiled Egg Mice

With a chive tail, radish ears, and olive eyes, a hard-boiled egg gets transformed into a whimsical mouse (that likes to be served a wedge of cheese, please).

Slice a peeled hard-boiled egg in half lengthwise. Place the halves yolk side down on a plate. Slice tiny black olive eyes and radish ears. Then make small slits in the egg halves for the eyes and ears and push in the olives and radishes. Add chive tails. Serve the pair of mice with a tiny wedge of Swiss cheese. Makes 2.

UFO Treats

I F YOUR KIDS are smitten with all things intergalactic, they'll love these spaceship snacks.

INGREDIENTS:
- ½ bagel
- 1 hard-boiled egg, peeled
  Cream cheese or peanut butter
  Carrot or banana slices
  Cheese slice

DIRECTIONS:
Spread the cream cheese or peanut butter on the bagel half, then set the peeled, hard-boiled egg in the center.

Decorate the ship with carrot or banana slices. Or, melt a slice of cheese on a bagel half before setting a hard-boiled egg in the center. Makes 1.

KIDS' STEPS: Kids can peel the eggs, spread the bagels with the cream cheese or peanut butter, and add the carrot or banana slices.

Prep time: 15 minutes

Deviled R-egg-atta

A SEAWORTHY TAKE on the classic picnic food, these cleverly engineered eggs are sure to become an instant favorite with your crew. Our tasters were egg-static over their mustardy zip and colorful sails.

INGREDIENTS:

    12 hard-boiled eggs
     2 teaspoons Dijon mustard
     2 teaspoons vinegar (white or
         cider)
    ¼ to ½ cup mayonnaise

     2 red, orange, yellow, or green
         bell peppers
         Paprika

DIRECTIONS:

Peel the eggs, then slice each one in half to make boats. Place the yolks in a medium-size bowl and mash them with a fork. Add the mustard and vinegar, then add the mayonnaise, stirring until the consistency is smooth but not soupy.

Next, make the sails. To do this, cut each pepper into 1-inch-wide strips, then cut the strips into 1-inch squares and slice each square in half diagonally.

Fill the egg-white halves with the yolk mixture. Stick the sail upright into the filling and sprinkle with paprika. Makes 2 dozen.

KIDS' STEPS: Kids can peel the eggs (keep an eye out for stray shell pieces!), pop out the yolks with a spoon, and mash the yolks with the other ingredients.

Prep time: 20 minutes

Bagel Critters

AT SNACK TIME, let your kids turn bagels, cream cheese, and assorted toppings into an edible zoo. This playful recipe also works well as an activity and quick lunch at a birthday party.

INGREDIENTS:

Bagels, sliced

Cream cheese, softened

Assorted toppings, such as baby carrots (grated or whole), cherry tomato halves, sliced black olives, sliced bell pepper (red, green, or yellow), poppy seeds, cucumber rounds, minced chives, and crunchy Chinese noodles

DIRECTIONS:

Spread the cream cheese on the cut bagels with a plastic knife.

Set out bowls of vegetables and crunchy noodles and let the kids turn the bagels into animal or monster faces like the royal lion (left) with olive eyes and nose, a crunchy noodle mane and whiskers, poppyseed freckles, and a pepper crown. The monster below is made with cucumber and olive eyes, baby-carrot hair and nose, and a red-pepper mouth. Make as many as you'd like.

KIDS' STEPS: Kids can spread the cream cheese with a plastic knife and turn the bagels into monsters and critters.

QUICK TRICK
Family Portrait Bagels

Celebrate your family by making a delicious, edible family portrait on bagels. Moms and dads can make their self-portraits on regular-size bagels; kids can create theirs on mini bagels.

Begin with a bagel covered with cream cheese. Next, create the family member's likeness with anything from blueberries and chocolate chips to tomatoes and chives. Set them together on a plate — and don't forget to take a family photo! Here's what we used:

MOM

Lox hair, black-olive eyes, parsley lashes, red-pepper lips, and a carrot nose.

GIRL

Carrot hair, chive hair ribbon, green-pepper eyes, chopped-peanut freckles, and grape-tomato mouth.

BOY

Chive hair, carrot-and-black-olive eyes, and tomato mouth.

Prep time: 15 minutes

Cookie-cutter Cheese Toasts

Kids like these treats because they look like cookies; parents like them because they aren't. Serve them warm or cold; they're terrific either way.

Heat the oven or toaster oven to 350°. Place 2 slices of whole-wheat bread on a cookie sheet or toaster-oven tray and top each with a slice of cheese. Cut out shapes using cookie cutters.

Place the "cookies" in the oven and heat until cheese melts. Serve warm or place in plastic bags when cool for a portable snack.

Butterfly Cheese-wich

BUTTERFLY FANS will flutter at the sight of this grilled cheese sandwich on their plates.

INGREDIENTS:
1 pat butter
2 slices bread
2 slices cheese
  Vegetables, such as celery, tomatoes, carrots, and peppers

DIRECTIONS:
Melt the pat of butter in a frying pan. Assemble and grill the sandwich as you would a regular grilled cheese, then cut out the wings as shown. Place a celery stick in the center for the butterfly's body, poke cherry tomatoes onto carrot sticks for antennae, then add carrot or pepper spots. Makes 1 butterfly.

KIDS' STEPS: Kids can cut the sandwich into wings with a plastic knife and create a butterfly body with vegetables.

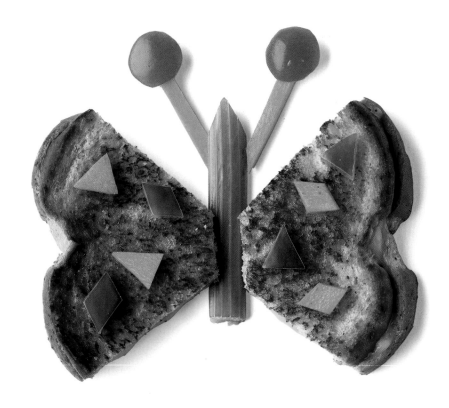

Prep time: 5 minutes   Cooking time: 5 minutes

Bob and Betty Bread

WHO SAYS ALL gingerbread people have to be made out of cookie dough? We use a slice of whole-wheat bread for this more healthful version.

INGREDIENTS:

1 to 2 slices of whole-wheat bread

Vegetables, such as peas, red and orange peppers, corn niblets, carrots, and cherry tomatoes

Parsley (optional)

DIRECTIONS:

From a slice of whole-wheat bread, cut out a gingerbread man or woman with a cookie cutter. If one slice isn't large enough, cut the top half from one slice and the bottom from another, then arrange the crusts at the waistband.

Dress up the folks with green pea buttons and red or orange pepper belts and shoes. Put on a happy face with corn-niblet eyes, a carrot nose, and a red-pepper smile. For a hat, use a quartered cherry tomato with a red-pepper brim. Or skip the hat and go for a head of curly parsley hair. Makes 1 or 2.

KIDS' STEPS: Kids can press the cookie cutter into the bread and decorate the cutouts with vegetables.

Prep time: 5 minutes

Spiral Sandwiches

KIDS WILL BE so proud of themselves when they create these elegant roll-ups that show off a food design inside. Give your young chefs lots of elbow room and tell them to take their time.

INGREDIENTS:

- ½ cup cream cheese, at room temperature
- 4 chives, 1 sprig of dill, and/or 3 basil leaves (optional)
- 6 spinach leaves
- 2 8- to 10-inch flour tortillas
- 1 tomato, seeded and sliced into thin rounds

DIRECTIONS:

Place the cream cheese in a small bowl. To make herbed cream cheese, snip the chives, dill, or basil into tiny pieces, then mash them into the cream cheese with the back of a spoon.

Spread a little cream cheese on each of the spinach leaves, then spread the remainder in a thin layer on the tortillas. Place three tomato slices in a row down the middle of each tortilla. Top with the spinach leaves, cream cheese facing up.

Roll up each tortilla tightly into a log. Pinch the ends shut. Use a serrated knife (slowly) to slice each log crosswise into 5 or 6 pinwheel sandwiches. Serves 2 to 4.

KIDS' STEPS: Kids can snip and mix the herbs into the cream cheese and layer the tortillas.

Prep time: 10 minutes

Cut It Out

Hundreds of *FamilyFun* readers transform their kids' sandwiches into fun food by slicing them with cookie cutters, including Mary Anne DeZur of Oshkosh, Wisconsin, who observed the following series of events: Day 1: Nutritious sandwich came back home — with one bite taken out of it. Day 2: Identical sandwich cut in a bear shape — gone. "Mom, we love that sandwich!" exclaimed her kids, Louie, six, and Sami, 10. "Can we have another tomorrow?"

Now Mary Anne incorporates the technique into her regular routine. She precuts all of her bread once a week and stores the shaped pieces in the freezer, ready for morning lunchmaking. The crusts she scatters outside for birds or dries in the oven and turns into bread crumbs.

After four years, she has amassed a huge collection of cookie cutters. She also has perfected her monthly strategy: three weeks of shaped sandwiches, followed by a week of regular sandwiches, "just so they really miss it."

Pita Rabbit

ONE LOOK AT this sweet, fluffy bunny snack, and your child will hop right up to the table.

INGREDIENTS:

1   small pita bread
    Marshmallow Fluff
    Peanut butter (optional)
    Strawberry or raspberry jam
    Pretzel sticks

DIRECTIONS:

Separate a small pita bread into two circles by inserting a butter knife between the layers from the outer edge and then carefully cutting around the circumference. Use one circle for the bunny's face and cut the other into halves for the ears.

Arrange the pieces, as shown, on a plate. Spread with Marshmallow Fluff (and peanut butter, if you like). With the butter knife, gently swirl a bit of jam into the Fluff to create a pink nose, mouth, and ears. Add two dollops of jam for eyes and pretzel sticks for whiskers. Makes 1.

KIDS' STEPS: Kids can spread the Fluff on the pita, swirl the jam into the Fluff, and make the bunny whiskers with the pretzels.

Prep time: 5 minutes

Lunch Guests

I F YOUR KIDS have ever stuck out their tongues at a snack you've prepared, here's your chance to turn the tables — by serving up a couple of cold-cut sandwiches that come with extra personality.

INGREDIENTS:

> Condiments, such as mustard or mayonnaise
> Sandwich rolls
> Cold cuts, such as ham, turkey, and roast beef
> Raw vegetables, such as olives, tomatoes, carrots, bell peppers, and cucumbers
> Cream cheese, softened
> Cheese cubes

DIRECTIONS:

Spread your child's favorite condiment on the bottom half of a sandwich roll. Add a slice of ham or another cold cut. Then fold a second slice of meat lengthwise so that it resembles a tongue, and lay it across the roll with one end hanging over the edge, as shown.

Place the top of the roll on the cold cuts and create a face on the bun top using sliced raw vegetables and olives for features and softened cream cheese for glue. (The cream cheese sticks best if you first blot dry the cut veggies with a paper towel.) You can even add a couple of cheese cube "teeth."

Use a vegetable peeler to create long carrot curls to pile on top of the sandwich or push bell pepper slices into the bun for a spiky hairdo.

KIDS' STEPS: Kids can spread the condiments on the bread and make the silly faces out of cold cuts and vegetables.

MY GREAT IDEA

Homemade Kids' Meals

"My kids enjoy getting a children's meal at the local fast-food restaurant, but this isn't always economical or practical. So now I make my own fast-food meals. While I'm fixing lunch, I let the children color a white paper lunch bag. Into this bag goes the meal: a sandwich or hot dog, a piece of fruit, crackers or chips, a straw, and a napkin. For the ever-popular toy, I save prizes from inside cereal boxes. I top off the bag with a juice box or a drink in a cup with a lid. The kids pretend to 'drive through' the kitchen, picking up their lunches at the counter. Not only is this idea affordable, but I can also make the meals healthy ones, and the kids have as much fun as if we went out."

— *Kathleen S. Bostrom*
Wildwood, Illinois

Assemble a Sub

TO PREVENT a soggy sub sandwich, pack up the fixings individually and let your young chef make a fresh sandwich at school.

INGREDIENTS:

Italian sandwich fillings, such as lettuce, black olives, onions, cherry tomatoes, provolone, and salami
Sub roll or baguette section
Italian dressing, mustard, or mayonnaise

DIRECTIONS:

First, prepare the fillings. Shred the lettuce, chop the olives, and slice the onions. Wash and dry the cherry tomatoes. Line up the vegetables in rows in a sealable plastic container. Roll up the provolone and the salami and place them in the container next to the veggies.

Pour Italian dressing into a small plastic container or add packets of mustard or mayonnaise.

In a lunch box, put the container with the fillings, the dressing, a sub roll wrapped in plastic, and a plastic knife (for slicing the tomatoes and spreading the mayonnaise or mustard).

At school, your child can build a sub or just eat the fillings as an antipasto. Makes 1.

KIDS' STEPS: Kids can roll up the cold cuts and cheese and pack them in the plastic container with the other sandwich fixings.

COOKING BASIC
Sandwich Sensations

Englishman John Montagu, Fourth Earl of Sandwich, is credited with inventing the sandwich when he needed a quick and easy meal. Still popular more than 200 years later, the sandwich lends itself to many tasty variations, including the following:

CALIFORNIA VEGGIE

Spread herbed cream cheese on multigrain bread, then add lettuce, tomato, grated carrot, alfalfa sprouts, and slices of avocado and cucumber.

FAJITA WRAP

Roll up strips of grilled chicken breast, salsa, refried beans, lettuce, and shredded pepper Jack cheese in a warm tortilla.

REUBEN

Pile hot corned beef or pastrami, Swiss cheese, and sauerkraut atop grilled rye bread and smother with Thousand Island dressing.

CAPE CODDER

Stack turkey, cranberry sauce, stuffing, lettuce, and red onion slices on marbled rye or pumpernickel bread.

Prep time: 10 minutes

Peanutty Drumsticks

MARINATED IN A mild peanut sauce, these golden-brown drumsticks taste sweet, with a hint of curry. Leftovers make a great school lunch.

INGREDIENTS:
- ½ cup peanut butter (creamy or crunchy)
- ⅓ cup honey
- ¼ cup soy sauce
- 3 tablespoons vegetable oil
- 1 teaspoon curry powder
- 1 garlic clove, minced
- 2½ pounds chicken drumettes, drumsticks, or wings

DIRECTIONS:
In a large mixing bowl, whisk together the peanut butter, honey, soy sauce, and oil until smooth. Then stir in the curry powder and the minced garlic.

Place the drumsticks in the marinade bowl and carefully stir until each piece is thoroughly coated. (Another technique is to shake the meat and marinade in a large sealable plastic bag.) Cover and refrigerate for at least 2 hours (but no more than 12 hours).

Heat the oven to 375°. Place the chicken pieces on a foil-lined baking sheet, discard the marinade, and bake for 25 to 30 minutes, or until the chicken is golden brown and the juices run clear.

Serve the drumsticks warm or cold. If your kids are taking these to school, pack them in an insulated lunch box with an ice pack — and provide plenty of napkins to wipe off gooey fingers. Serves 4 to 6.

QUICK TRICK
Cold Cut Puzzler

Let your child play with her food with this puzzle of a sandwich. Start by making a sandwich with bologna (or another favorite deli meat) and cheese slices on white, whole-wheat, or sourdough bread. Cut the sandwich into a number of imaginative shapes, then separate the shapes and place them, mixed up, on her lunch plate. Have your child reconstruct her sandwich by fitting together the puzzle pieces before she eats them.

KIDS' STEPS: Kids can measure and mix the marinade, stir the drumsticks in it, and use tongs to place them on the baking sheet.

Prep time: 15 minutes   Marinating time: 2 hours
Cooking time: 15 to 30 minutes

Perfect Pesto

This versatile sauce can be tossed in pasta, served as a veggie dip, or used as a sandwich spread.

2½ to 3 cups lightly packed fresh basil leaves

2 garlic cloves, peeled

½ cup extra-virgin olive oil

¼ cup pine nuts or walnuts
   Big pinch of salt

½ to ¾ cup freshly grated Parmesan cheese

Rinse and dry the basil, then put it in a food processor along with the garlic cloves, olive oil, pine nuts or walnuts, and salt. Process the mixture until fairly smooth, stopping occasionally to scrape down the sides with a rubber spatula.

Transfer the mixture to a small bowl and stir in the Parmesan cheese. Store any leftover pesto in the refrigerator or, if you're not planning to use it within 2 weeks, in the freezer. To keep the pesto from turning brown, place a piece of plastic wrap directly onto the sauce before storing. Makes 1 cup.

Pesto, Cheese, and Chicken Melt

PESTO is so delicious, kids are willing to try it on just about anything, like this grilled cheese and chicken sandwich. You can use store-bought pesto, of course, but it's great fun to make it from scratch (see recipe at left).

INGREDIENTS:

2 slices fresh Italian bread (about ¾ inch thick)

2 tablespoons pesto (see left)

2 slices provolone or sharp Cheddar cheese

2 or 3 thin slices deli chicken or turkey

2 or 3 thin slices ripe tomato (optional)

1 tablespoon butter, softened

DIRECTIONS:

On each bread slice, spread 1 tablespoon of the pesto. Then build the sandwich on one of the slices, first layering on 1 slice of cheese and then all of the chicken or turkey. Add the tomato if you're using it, then the second slice of cheese. Press the other piece of bread, pesto side down, onto the sandwich.

Use a paper towel to rub an unheated heavy skillet with a little cooking oil. Place the skillet over moderate heat. Meanwhile, spread the softened butter on both sides of the sandwich. Carefully place the sandwich in the heated pan and grill it on each side for about 3 to 3½ minutes, until golden brown.

Using a spatula, transfer the sandwich to a cutting board and slice it in half before serving. Makes 1.

KIDS' STEPS: Kids can spread the pesto on the bread and layer the sandwich with the cheese, the chicken or turkey, and the tomato.

Prep time: 5 minutes Cooking time: 7 minutes

Veggie Quesadillas

KIDS LOVE QUESADILLAS because they're a vehicle for cheese, parents love them because they also contain nutritious vegetables. Couple your quesadilla with the salsa and guacamole on page 39, if you like.

INGREDIENTS:

¼ cup grated carrot

¼ cup cooked and chopped broccoli

1 tablespoon chopped yellow or Vidalia onion (optional)

⅓ cup shredded Monterey Jack or Cheddar cheese

½ teaspoon canola oil

1 10-inch (burrito-style) flour tortilla

1 tablespoon salsa or taco sauce

DIRECTIONS:

In a medium-size bowl, mix the carrot, broccoli, onion (if desired), and cheese. Set a large nonstick frying pan over medium heat and thinly coat the bottom of the pan with canola oil. Place a tortilla in the pan, cover it with the cheese-veggie mixture, and drizzle the salsa or taco sauce on top. When the bottom of the tortilla is lightly browned and the cheese has melted, fold the quesadilla in half and transfer it to a plate. Cut it into quarters and serve hot. Serves 2.

KIDS' STEPS: Kids can mix the vegetables and cheese together.

Simple Stromboli

"Whenever time is short and I have leftover cold cuts, I roll up this delicious stromboli.

"Simply roll out and flatten a 10-ounce package of pizza crust dough onto a greased 9- by 13-inch pan. Bake at 350° until the dough starts to rise a little but is still flexible enough to roll (about 5 minutes).

"Remove the pan from the oven and cover the dough with layers of your favorite meats and cheeses, leaving 1 to 2 inches uncovered on one of the short sides of the pan. Starting from the other short side, roll the dough up. Place the stromboli seam-side down in the middle of the pan, brush with a little oil, and cook until brown, about 25 to 35 minutes. Cool before slicing.

"I've served this stromboli warm, cold, and at room temperature — for dinner, lunch, and snack — and it always receives rave reviews!"

—*Mary Patten*

Hopkinton, Massachusetts

Prep time: 10 minutes Cooking time: 5 minutes

Peanut Butter Bugs

High-protein critters are just one of the many sculptures your kids can form out of this peanut butter play clay.

To make up a batch, mix $\frac{1}{4}$ cup creamy peanut butter, 1 tablespoon wheat germ, 1 tablespoon honey, and 3 tablespoons nonfat dried milk in a bowl until it sticks together. Chill, then model the clay into a ladybug or a snail, and add shoestring licorice features and raisin eyes. Once playtime is over, kids can gobble their creatures up.

Peanut Butter and Jelly Stars

THERE'S NO DOUBT that PB&J has star status among kids. Our version dresses up the classic sandwich by punching star shapes out of the bread.

INGREDIENTS:

- 1 1½-inch star cookie cutter (available at kitchen- and party-supply stores)
- 2 slices white bread
- 2 slices whole-wheat bread
   Peanut butter
   Jelly

DIRECTIONS:

Using the star cookie cutter, cut two stars out of each slice of the white bread and two stars out of each slice of the whole-wheat bread. Then fit the whole-wheat stars into the star-shaped holes in the white bread and the white stars into the whole-wheat bread.

Spread on the peanut butter and jelly, working slowly to avoid tearing the bread, and assemble. Makes 2 star-studded sandwiches.

KIDS' STEPS: Kids can press cookie cutters into the bread and carefully spread peanut butter and jelly on the bread.

Prep time: 5 minutes

PB&J Pizza

FOR A QUICK lunch or after-school snack, invite your kids to assemble this no-cook "pizza." Like its cheesy cousin, this one can be customized with favorite toppings.

INGREDIENTS:

   3 tablespoons peanut butter (creamy or crunchy)

   3 tablespoons jelly

   1 whole pita bread (medium-size)

      Toppings, such as raisins, Cheerios, apple slices, banana slices, and peanuts

DIRECTIONS:

Spread the peanut butter and jelly "sauce" on the pita bread. Then top the pizza with your child's favorite goodies — raisins, Cheerios, apple slices, banana slices, and/or peanuts. Arrange the toppings randomly or in a pattern. Use a pizza cutter to slice the pizza into 4 wedges. Serve with a tall glass of milk. Serves 1 to 2.

KIDS' STEPS: Kids can put the toppings on the pizza and slice it with a pizza cutter (see below).

TIP: The best way to use a pizza cutter is to grip the handle firmly, apply slight pressure, and roll the blade steadily and in a straight line. This tool can also be used to cut cookie dough, sandwich bread, and quesadillas (or real pizza).

COOKING BASIC

Homemade Peanut Butter

For a fun after-school activity, help your child use a food processor to mix up peanut butter from scratch.

   2 cups unsalted dry-roasted peanuts

   3 to 4 tablespoons vegetable oil

   ¼ teaspoon salt

Pour the peanuts into the bowl of a food processor. Process until they are finely chopped. Add the vegetable oil 1 tablespoon at a time, processing until the peanut butter begins to form a ball. Add the salt and process until well combined. Transfer to a clean jar with a lid. Decorate a large white mailing label before affixing it to the jar. Makes 1 cup. Store in the refrigerator for up to 2 weeks.

Prep time: 10 minutes

Spider Pretzel

These arachnid treats are easy to make — and they look positively lifelike crawling across your child's snack plate.

- 2 round crackers
- 2 teaspoons creamy peanut butter
- 8 small pretzel sticks
- 2 raisins

With the peanut butter, make a cracker sandwich. Insert eight pretzel "legs" into the filling. With a dab of peanut butter, set two raisin "eyes" on top. Makes 1 edible spider.

Shrunken Sandwich

PRESCHOOLERS LOVE miniature things — tiny plastic dinosaurs, small baby dolls, and wee snacks. These shrunken sandwiches are just the right size to share with stuffed animals.

INGREDIENTS:
- 2 slices ham
- 2 slices cheese
- 12 mini crackers, such as Ritz Bits

DIRECTIONS:
Cut the ham and cheese into small rounds the size of the mini crackers. You can use tiny cookie cutters or a clean bottle top. Place a ham round on six of the crackers, then a cheese round. Cover each with another cracker. Serves 2.

KIDS' STEPS: Kids can cut out the ham and cheese with tiny cookie cutters or clean bottle tops and assemble the shrunken sandwiches.

Prep time: 10 minutes

Whole-wheat House

LET YOUR BUILDER-to-be help construct a house out of toast for a morning snack.

INGREDIENTS:

2 pieces of toast
Mini-wheat cereal
Peanut butter
Cheerios

DIRECTIONS:
Use one piece of toast for the house, cutting out the windows and door. To raise the roof, cut the second piece into a triangle and shingle it with the mini-wheat cereal held in place with peanut butter. A small rectangle of toast, cut to fit against the roofline, makes an ideal chimney, especially with a puff of Cheerios smoke. For siding, spread the whole house with peanut butter, scratching in some shingles with a toothpick or fork. Makes 1.

KIDS' STEPS: Kids can shingle the roof with mini-wheat cereal and make the chimney smoke with Cheerios.

QUICK TRICK
Zoo Sandwich

Kids can make their own three-dimensional zoo using animal crackers. Give each child 2 crackers of the same animal. Have them spread on jam or peanut butter to make cracker sandwiches. Stand the crackers up and parade them across the table.

Prep time: 10 minutes

CHAPTER FOUR

Sweet Treats

SOMETIMES SWEETNESS sends out its irresistible siren song, and your kids get a powerful urge for sugary treats. As long as kids eat a balanced diet, go ahead and indulge this craving every now and then — it may even be their body's way of announcing a sagging energy level. But instead of buying a packaged sweet nothing, bake one of our treats. Not only will these satisfy a sweet tooth, but they'll also fill a rainy afternoon, or get your kids hooked on cooking. Flip through this chapter and you'll find a sweet something that's sure to please both you and your kids.

Turn your kids into kitchen artists. Many of our recipes offer all the creative fun of an art project with the satisfaction of a sweet to eat. Help your kids create an edible masterpiece, such as our Cookie Paintings (page 84), Ice-cream Pizza (page 88), or Cookie Puppets (page 85).

Make it dessert. Most of the recipes in this chapter — from the erupting ice-cream volcano (page 86) to the tamer Berry Apple Crisp (page 77) or Giant Cowboy Cookies (page 80) — can moonlight as perfectly delicious desserts. If you want leftovers for lunch box take-alongs or next-day snacking, simply double the recipe.

Bring a sweet snack to a school or scout function. Is it your turn to bring dessert to the school's bake sale or scout meeting? Make The Shamburgers (page 83), the Flower Cupcakes (page 91), or the Mock Sushi (page 92), and you'll be the talk of the town. Or volunteer to bring the ingredients into your child's classroom and cook up an edible science (and art) project.

Make the most of your freezer. When it comes to kids, even the simplest frozen treats mean good, frosty fun. Our frozen Ice-cream Sandwiches (page 86) can be made in bulk and stored in the freezer. You can also make and freeze a big batch of our Cookie Dough (page 84) to have on hand for impromptu cookie-baking sessions. By spending a few minutes on prep and presentation, you can craft a frozen treat to rival anything from the ice-cream parlor!

Offer fruit as a sweet treat. When it comes to snacking, fruit can hold its own against even the toughest competitors: it's sweet, it's juicy, and it comes in its own colorful wrapper! Keep a bowl of washed fruit on the counter or in the fridge where it will present a temptingly healthful, easily transportable snack. Or make one of our fast fruit treats — a Waffle Butterfly (page 77) or Watermelon Sherbet Smoothies (page 79) — for a colorful, nutritious snack.

Crispy Rice Pops, page 93

Chocolate-dipped Strawberries

Dunked in melted chocolate, fresh strawberries look elegant and taste divine. Wash and pat dry 1 pint of strawberries. Melt 4 ounces of Baker's German's Sweet Chocolate in the microwave for 1 to 2 minutes, then stir until smooth. Dip each strawberry in the chocolate, then place on waxed paper until the chocolate has cooled. Enjoy!

Cheery Cherry Cheesecakes

WHILE FRESH cherries on their own make a perfect snack, you just can't beat the taste of them as a topping on these mini cheesecakes.

INGREDIENTS:

CRUST:

   5   whole chocolate graham crackers
   2   tablespoons sugar
   2   tablespoons butter, melted

FILLING:

   1   8-ounce package cream cheese, softened
  ¼   cup sugar
   1   egg
  ¼   teaspoon vanilla extract
  ¼   cup sour cream
  ¼   cup whipping cream

TOPPING:

   3   dozen fresh cherries
   1   to 2 teaspoons sugar
       Whipped cream (optional)

DIRECTIONS:

Heat the oven to 300°. Line a 12-cup muffin tin with aluminum baking cups, then coat the cups with cooking spray.

Place the graham crackers in a sturdy plastic bag and use a rolling pin to crush them. Pour the cracker crumbs into a medium-size bowl, then stir in the sugar and melted butter. Place a rounded tablespoon of the crumb mixture into each of the muffin cups, then use the bottom of a small cup to press the crumbs flat.

In a large bowl, use an electric mixer to beat together the cream cheese and sugar until smooth, then beat in the egg and vanilla extract. With a spatula or wooden spoon, add the sour cream and whipping cream, stirring until combined, then pour the mixture onto the crusts.

Bake the cheesecakes for 25 minutes. Allow them to cool completely at room temperature, then chill them in the refrigerator until you're ready to serve them.

For the topping, slice each cherry into fourths, removing the pit. Place the cherry slices in a small bowl and add 1 to 2 teaspoons of sugar, stirring until the sugar is dissolved.

Just before serving, top each mini cheesecake with approximately 12 cherry slices and a dollop of whipped cream. Serves 12.

KIDS' STEPS: Kids can use a rolling pin to crush the graham crackers, measure the filling ingredients, and add the cherries to the cheesecakes.

Prep time: 20 minutes   Baking time: 25 minutes

Strawberry Shortcake Snake

STRAWBERRY SEASON is no time to scale back on dessert — particularly if one of these shortcake snakes winds up on your plate.

INGREDIENTS:

- 2 cups all-purpose flour
- 6 tablespoons confectioners' sugar, plus extra for berries
- 4 teaspoons baking powder
- ¾ teaspoon salt
- ½ cup (1 stick) margarine
- ¾ cup milk
- 1 quart strawberries
  Whipped cream, mini M&M's, and green fruit leather

DIRECTIONS:

Heat the oven to 400°. Sift together the flour, 2 tablespoons of the confectioners' sugar, baking powder, and salt into a large mixing bowl. Cut in the margarine with a pastry cutter. Once the dough is crumbly, slowly stir in the milk.

Turn out the dough onto a floured working surface and gently roll or pat the dough into a 1-inch-thick rectangle (it should measure about 6 by 8 inches). For the best results, handle the dough as little as possible.

Slice the rectangle into four 1½- by 8-inch strips. Place the strips on an ungreased baking sheet, then mold and curve them into S shapes to resemble snakes. Bake for 10 to 12 minutes, until the bottoms are golden brown. Transfer the baked shortcakes to a wire rack and let cool.

Slice all but 4 of the berries lengthwise into a mixing bowl. Toss with the remaining confectioners' sugar.

Slice the cooled shortcakes in half lengthwise, arrange the sliced strawberries on the bottom half of each one, then cover with the shortcake top. Cover the tops with whipped cream and sliced strawberry "scales." Add a whole strawberry head, M&M's eyes, and a fruit-leather tongue. Serves 4.

KIDS' STEPS: Kids can help shape the shortcake into curvy bodies and embellish the strawberry heads with candy eyes and forked tongues.

Prep time: 25 minutes Baking time: 12 minutes

Berry Apple Crisp

THIS RECIPE combines late summer berries and fall apples into a dessert your family will polish off in no time.

INGREDIENTS:

- 6 tablespoons butter, softened
- ⅔ cup rolled oats
- ⅓ cup all-purpose flour
- ⅔ cup brown sugar
- 4 cups peeled apples, thinly sliced
- 1 teaspoon cinnamon
- ¼ teaspoon ground nutmeg
- 1 cup raspberries
  Ice cream (optional)

DIRECTIONS:

Heat the oven to 350°. In a bowl, blend the butter, oats, flour, and brown sugar with your fingertips until the mixture resembles crumbly cookie dough.

In a separate bowl, toss the apples and spices, then gently stir in the berries.

Turn the fruit into a greased 8-inch-square baking dish and top with the oat mixture. Bake for 30 to 35 minutes until the fruit is bubbling and the crust is golden. Serve with ice cream. Makes 4 to 6 servings.

KIDS' STEPS: Kids can mix up the crumb topping and toss the apples, raspberries, and spices.

QUICK TRICK
Waffle Butterfly

Your family can have fun adding a fruity flair to a breakfast favorite. Toast two round waffles and cut them each in half. Arrange the pieces around a banana for the insect's body, as shown. Add kiwi antennae and decorate the wings with slices of kiwi, strawberries, and banana. Serve with a drizzle of maple syrup. Serves 1.

Prep time: 20 minutes Baking time: 35 minutes

The Shamburger

SURE, IT LOOKS like the real thing. But when your kids take a bite, their taste buds will be pleasantly deceived by the no-beef patties, special sauce, and sesame cookie buns. And while they're not exactly fast food, these fake burgers are easy to make.

INGREDIENTS:

- 1 cup (2 sticks) margarine
- 1 cup sugar
- 3 eggs (1 is for the cookie glaze)
- 1 teaspoon vanilla extract
- 2½ cups all-purpose flour
- 1½ teaspoons baking powder
- ½ teaspoon salt
- 2 tablespoons sesame seeds
- 1 cup shredded coconut
  Green food coloring
  Red and yellow icing
- 12 large (1.5 ounces) or 36 medium (.6 ounce) peppermint patties

DIRECTIONS:

To make the cookie "hamburger buns," heat the oven to 375°. Use an electric mixer to cream the margarine and the sugar until fluffy (about 1 to 2 minutes). Add 2 eggs and beat well. Stir in the vanilla extract. Sift the flour, baking powder, and salt into a separate bowl. Then, add the dry ingredients to the creamed mixture and blend well.

For large "buns," drop the dough by rounded tablespoons onto a lightly greased baking sheet at least 1 inch apart (for medium-size buns, drop the dough by rounded teaspoons). Next, use the bottom of a floured glass to lightly press the dough into a circle. Then beat the remaining egg and use a pastry brush to "paint" it on top of each cookie. Sprinkle sesame seeds on the tops. Bake the large cookies for 10 minutes and the medium ones for 8 minutes, or until the cookies are golden brown.

While the cookies are cooling on a rack, make the "lettuce." Place the shredded coconut into a plastic bag. Add a few drops of green food coloring, close the bag, and shake until the coconut has turned a light green.

To assemble the burgers, choose two cookies that are about the same size and shape. Spread icing ketchup or mustard on the bottom bun, add an appropriately sized peppermint patty, and sprinkle with coconut lettuce. Add a squirt of icing ketchup or mustard to hold the top bun in place.

Arrange the hamburgers on a platter or wrap in foil. Makes approximately 12 large or 36 medium burgers.

KIDS' STEPS: Kids can shape the cookie dough buns, tint the coconut lettuce, and assemble the fake burgers.

QUICK TRICK

Burgers and Dogs

For an even faster pretend burger (and a hot dog, too!), try these sweet treats. You can serve them individually on plates or on frosted cupcakes.

BURGERS

Start with an upside-down vanilla wafer. With a dab of frosting, attach a Keebler Grasshopper cookie. Add a squirt of yellow-frosting mustard, red-frosting ketchup, and tinted coconut for lettuce. Top with the second vanilla wafer. Rub the top bun with orange-juice concentrate, then sprinkle with sesame seeds.

DOGS

First, make the hot dog bun by cutting a wedge out of a circus peanut. Roll a caramel square into a hot-dog shape in your hand. Place the hot dog in the bun and squirt on a squiggly line of yellow-frosting mustard. Garnish with green-gumdrop relish, if you wish.

Prep time: 30 minutes Baking time: 10 minutes

Cookie Dough

This recipe makes a sturdy sugar-cookie canvas just right for painting our cookies, puppets, and stars (shown at right and on page 85).

2 ¾   cups all-purpose flour

¾   teaspoon baking soda

½   teaspoon salt

1   cup (2 sticks) butter, at room temperature

1   cup sugar

1   large egg

1   tablespoon vanilla extract

Mix the flour, baking soda, and salt together and set aside. In a large bowl, cream the butter and sugar with an electric mixer. Add the egg and vanilla extract and mix until well combined.

Gradually add the flour mixture to the creamed mixture, mixing well after each addition. (The dough will be stiff.) Then roll the dough into two balls, flatten into disks, cover, and chill for at least 2 hours or overnight.

Once chilled, place each disk between two sheets of plastic wrap and roll out to a ¼-inch thickness. Remove the plastic and cut out shapes with a cookie cutter. Bake at 350° on a cookie sheet for 8 to 12 minutes, or until the edges begin to brown. Leave the cookies on the sheet for 2 minutes, then transfer them to a cooling rack. Makes about 34 3-inch cookies.

Cookie Paintings

EGG YOLKS AND food coloring make paints that look shiny and vibrant when baked on a cookie canvas.

INGREDIENTS:

4   eggs
     Food coloring
     Small-tip paintbrushes
     Cookie dough, either store-bought or the recipe at left

DIRECTIONS:
To make the egg-yolk paint, first separate one egg and discard the white. Then, pour the yolk into a cup and beat it with a fork until smooth. Add 5 or 6 drops of food coloring and beat until the color is evenly distributed. Repeat with the remaining eggs and colors.

Roll out the cookie dough to a ¼-inch thickness between two pieces of plastic. Remove the top piece and, with a butter knife, cut out 3½- by 5-inch rectangle canvases.

Using the paints and a brush, paint any design you like — a landscape, an animal, or an abstract design. Chill the dough until firm. Transfer cookies to a baking sheet.

Bake at 350° for 8 to 12 minutes, or until the edges begin to brown. Let set on the baking sheet for 2 minutes, then transfer to racks to cool. Makes 8 to 12 cookies.

KIDS' STEPS: Kids can roll out the dough and paint their cookies.

Prep time: 15 minutes   Baking time: 12 minutes
Chill time: 30 minutes

Cookie Puppets

A TOP A LOLLIPOP stick and decorated with candies, the classic sugar cookie quickly becomes a great entertainer.

INGREDIENTS:

    Cookie dough, either store-bought or homemade (page 84), chilled
15 to 18 lollipop sticks
    Frosting (see page 91)
    Assorted candies

DIRECTIONS:

Place the cookie dough on a large piece of plastic wrap, cover with another piece of plastic wrap, and then roll the dough until it is ¼ inch thick. Lift off the top sheet of plastic wrap and use a widemouthed glass (about 3½ inches in diameter) to cut out 15 to 18 faces for the cookie puppets.

Place each cookie on an ungreased baking sheet and press a lollipop stick in the center. To ensure that the cookies hold their shape, chill for another 30 minutes. Repeat the process with the remaining dough.

While the dough is chilling, heat the oven to 350°. Bake the cookies for 8 to 12 minutes or until golden brown around the edges. Cool on the baking sheets for 5 minutes and then remove to cooling racks.

To add features to the puppets, fill a pastry bag with frosting and use a writing tip to add eyes, a mouth, and a mop of hair. Set out assorted candies and use dabs of the frosting to attach such goodies as fruit slice lips, hard candy eyes, candy orange slice ears, or lace licorice hair — whatever candy features you think look best.

The cookie puppets won't last long, but if you have any left over, store them in an airtight container between waxed paper. Makes 15 to 18 puppets.

QUICK TRICK
Cookie Constellation

Let the stars come out at your next picnic — use a batch of store-bought or homemade (see page 84) cookie dough to make star-shaped cookies. Then bake according to recipe directions. Decorate the cooled cookies with white frosting and sprinkle on edible glitter (sold at most party supply stores).

KIDS' STEPS: Kids can measure dry ingredients, roll out cookie dough, cut out the cookies, and help decorate them.

Prep time: 15 minutes Baking time: 12 minutes

QUICK TRICK

Frosty Flow

Serve one of these ice-cream volca-noes to a group of kids, and you'll be lucky if the strawberry lava reaches the serving dish before it's all scooped up.

To create one, simply invert an opened half-gallon tub-style container of chocolate ice cream onto a large plate and cut or peel away the container. Allow the ice cream to soften for a few minutes, then use a spoon or butter knife to shape the mountaintop into a peak. Sprinkle on plenty of chocolate cookie-crumb gravel and spoon sliced strawberries in syrup over the top, coaxing some to flow down the sides.

Ice-cream Sandwiches

HERE'S THE SCOOP on how to make ice-cream sandwiches from scratch. The results are worth the effort: the finished product looks like store-bought ice-cream sandwiches but tastes even better.

INGREDIENTS:
- ½ cup (1 stick) margarine
- 1 cup packed brown sugar
- 2 eggs
- 1 teaspoon vanilla extract
- ½ cup cocoa powder
- 2 cups all-purpose flour
- 1 teaspoon baking powder
- ¼ teaspoon salt
  Half-gallon carton vanilla ice cream

DIRECTIONS:
In a medium-size bowl, cream the margarine and brown sugar. Beat in the eggs, one at a time, then the vanilla extract.

In a separate bowl, stir together the cocoa, flour, baking powder, and salt. Gradually add the dry ingredi-ents to the margarine mixture. Beat until well combined. Gather the dough into a ball, wrap with plastic, and chill for at least 1 hour.

Heat the oven to 375°. On a lightly floured surface, roll out the dough to ¼-inch thickness. Use a ruler and a sharp knife to cut out rectangular pieces, about 2¼ by 5 inches.

Transfer the rectangles to an un-greased baking sheet. Use the tines of a fork to make patterns on the cookies.

Bake the cookies for 8 to 10 minutes or until set. Cool.

Meanwhile, cut rectangular blocks from the ice cream. To do this, peel back the half-gallon carton and cut ½-inch-thick slabs that are roughly the dimensions of your baked cookies. Freeze the blocks.

Once the cookies have thoroughly cooled, place one ice-cream block between two cookies. Trim the sides with a knife, wrap the sandwich in foil, and freeze for several hours. Repeat until you have used all the cookies and ice cream. Makes enough dough for 6 large sandwiches.

KIDS' STEPS: Kids can measure and mix ingredients for the chocolate sandwich dough and decorate the dough with the tines of a fork.

Prep time: 25 minutes Chilling time: 1 hour
Baking time: 10 minutes Freezing time: 3 hours

Ice-cream Cookie Cups

WANT TO HAVE your cookies and ice cream, too? You can with these edible cookie bowls.

INGREDIENTS:
- ¼ cup shortening
- ¼ cup (½ stick) butter, softened
- ⅔ cup sugar
- 1 egg
- ½ teaspoon vanilla extract
- 1½ cups all-purpose flour
- ½ teaspoon salt
- ¼ teaspoon baking powder
- ¼ cup miniature semisweet chocolate chips
- Ice cream

DIRECTIONS:

Beat the shortening, butter, and sugar in a large bowl. Add the egg and vanilla extract, beating until combined. In a separate bowl, sift together the flour, salt, and baking powder, then gradually stir them into the batter. Stir in the chocolate chips.

Divide the dough in half, shape each half into a flat disk, and wrap it in plastic. Chill the dough in the refrigerator for at least 2 hours.

Heat the oven to 375°. Turn two 12-cup muffin tins bottom side up and cover 10 of the cup bottoms with squares of aluminum foil (use every other cup so there's space between them). Grease the foil with shortening and set it aside.

Unwrap 1 disk of dough, place it between 2 sheets of waxed paper, and roll it out to an ⅛-inch thickness. Cut out circles of dough 4 inches around and place each one over a muffin cup bottom, smoothing out any cracks. Repeat with the other disk, rerolling and reusing any scraps.

Bake the cookie cups for 10 to 12 minutes or until light brown. Let them cool for 10 minutes, then remove the foil and cookies together from the muffin pan. Peel off the foil and let the cups cool completely on a rack. Just before serving, fill each cookie cup with a scoop of ice cream. Makes 10.

KIDS' STEPS: Kids can measure and mix up the ingredients for the cookie cups, then fill the baked cups with their favorite ice cream.

Prep time: 20 minutes   Chilling time: 2 hours   Baking time: 12 minutes

Ice-cream Pizza

IMAGINE AN OVERSIZE ice-cream sandwich with only one cookie — a delicious brownie cookie. Now pretend you get to divide the sandwich into slices and decorate each with piles of whipped cream and colorful candies. The best part? It's no fantasy. It's our Cookie-crusted Ice-cream Pizza, and it's a snap to make.

INGREDIENTS:

- 4 tablespoons butter
- 3 ounces unsweetened chocolate, coarsely chopped
- 1 cup sugar
- 2 eggs, at room temperature
- 1 teaspoon vanilla extract
- ½ cup finely chopped walnut or pecan pieces
- 1 cup all-purpose flour
- 1½ teaspoons baking powder
- ¼ teaspoon salt
- ½ gallon ice cream (we like strawberry for pizza color)
- Canned whipped cream
- Various decorative candies

DIRECTIONS:

Line a large cookie sheet with aluminum foil. Lightly butter the foil and set it aside.

Melt together the butter and chocolate in a double boiler (or in the microwave on medium, stirring every 30 seconds), stirring until smooth. Set aside to cool.

Using an electric mixer and a large bowl, beat the sugar and eggs on high speed for 5 minutes, until very airy. Blend in the melted chocolate and vanilla extract until smooth. Stir in the nuts. In a separate bowl, mix together the flour, baking powder, and salt. Add them to the chocolate mixture and stir until evenly blended. Let the dough sit for 2 to 3 minutes.

Scrape the dough into the center of the buttered foil. Using a fork, spread the dough into a more or less level circle 12 inches in diameter. Refrigerate it for 10 minutes while the oven heats to 350°.

Bake the crust for 13 minutes. Transfer it to a cooling rack and cool it until it is just warm to the touch. Invert the crust onto a second cookie sheet, then gently peel off the foil. Invert it again onto the original sheet or onto a serving tray and refrigerate for 30 minutes.

Soften the ice cream slightly before spreading it on the crust. Using an ice-cream paddle, smooth a layer of ice cream ½ to 1 inch thick evenly over the crust. Decorate using the canned whipped cream and candies (if you're presenting the pizza whole, consider using lines of whipped cream to draw slices). Transfer the pizza to the freezer until you're ready to slice and serve. Makes 6 to 8 servings.

KIDS' STEPS: Kids can help measure and mix ingredients for the cookie crust, and decorate the pizza with whipped cream and candies.

Prep time: 40 minutes Baking time: 13 minutes Cooling time: 60 minutes

Frog Cupcake

MAKING SILLY cupcakes is a great way to turn around a gray day. Bake up a batch of cupcakes either from a mix or your favorite recipe. Then let your kids turn them into irresistible frogs (or flowers at right).

INGREDIENTS:

1 baked cupcake
Blue frosting
1 large green gumdrop
2 white chocolate chips
Black decorators' icing

DIRECTIONS:
First, cover the cupcake with the blue frosting. Slice the large green gumdrop in half. Press the tip of a white chocolate chip into the cut surface of each half, centering it near the bottom edge. Squirt a dab of black decorators' icing onto each chip. Then press the frog eyes into the frosting. Makes 1.

KIDS' STEPS: Kids can frost and decorate the cupcakes with gumdrop eyes.

Prep time: 10 minutes

Flower Cupcake

THIS SWEET wildflower cup-cake is sure to be a favorite pick on a summery day.

INGREDIENTS:

1 baked cupcake
  Yellow frosting
1 gumdrop
2 marshmallows

DIRECTIONS:
Frost the cupcake with yellow frosting and place a colored gum-drop in the center. Next, set a large marshmallow on its side, press it flat with your palm, then cut it in thirds with kitchen scissors. Repeat with a second marshmallow and arrange the petals around the gum-drop center. Makes 1.

KIDS' STEPS: Kids can frost the cupcake and arrange gumdrop and marsh-mallow petals on it.

COOKING BASIC
Cupcake and Cookie Frosting

With this buttercream frosting, you can squirt letters and numbers, or facial features on your cupcakes or cookies. Cream 1 stick of softened butter and 3 cups of confectioners' sugar. Add 1 teaspoon of vanilla extract and 3 tablespoons of milk, then blend until smooth. Mix in desired food coloring. Spoon into a pastry bag and start decorating.

Prep time: 10 minutes

Mock Sushi

THERE'S DEFINITELY something fishy about these Japanese-style rolls. The rice filling is crispy, the wraps are fruity, and your kids will love them — no fooling!

INGREDIENTS:

  ¼ cup (½ stick) butter
  4 cups mini marshmallows
  6 cups crisped rice cereal
20 to 25 gummy worms
  1 to 2 boxes Fruit Roll-Ups

DIRECTIONS:

Grease a 12- by 17-inch baking sheet. Melt the butter in a large saucepan over low heat. Add the marshmallows and stir until smooth. Remove the mixture from the heat and stir in the rice cereal until it's evenly coated. Turn the baking sheet so that the shorter ends are at the top and bottom. Then press the marshmallow mixture onto the sheet, distributing it evenly.

While the mixture is still warm, place gummy worms on it from end to end, starting at one side an inch up from the lower edge. Gently roll the lower edge of the marshmallow mixture over the gummy worms. Then cut the log away from the rest of the mixture. Use the same method to form 4 more logs. Slice each log into 1-inch-thick "sushi" rolls and wrap them individually with a strip of Fruit Roll-Ups. Makes 4 to 5 dozen.

KIDS' STEPS: Kids can add the gummy worms, roll up the crispy rice logs, and wrap the individual pieces of sushi with the Fruit Roll-Up strips.

Prep time: 15 minutes   Cooking time: 15 minutes

Crispy Rice Pops

FOR A SNACK you can sell at a bake sale, try these crunchy, chocolaty lollipops. *FamilyFun* reader Shelley Kotulka came up with this novel twist on the bake sale classic for a craft fair in Wind Gap, Pennsylvania, and her treats sold out in no time.

INGREDIENTS:

- 3 tablespoons butter
- 1 10-ounce package regular marshmallows, or 4 cups mini marshmallows
- 6 to 7 cups crisped rice cereal
- 12 Popsicle sticks
- 1½ cups semisweet or white chocolate
  Sprinkles

DIRECTIONS:

In a large saucepan, melt the margarine over low heat. Add the marshmallows, stirring constantly until melted. Remove the pan from the heat and stir in the cereal until it's well coated.

Let the mixture cool until it's warm but comfortable to handle with your fingers. Lightly butter your hands, then shape the treats into 12 balls. Push a Popsicle stick into each one. Set aside to cool.

Meanwhile, melt the chocolate in a metal bowl set over a pan of hot, but not boiling, water. Dip the marshmallow treats into the melted chocolate and add the sprinkles. Set the lollipops on a waxed paper–lined tray. Once the chocolate has hardened, wrap the treats in plastic and tie with a ribbon. Makes 12.

KIDS' STEPS: Kids can shape the slightly cooled crispy rice mix into balls, push in Popsicle sticks, and dip them in the melted chocolate and sprinkles.

QUICK TRICK
Rocky Road Fudge

Whip up homemade fudge in a matter of minutes. Simply melt one 12-ounce package of chocolate chips in a double boiler or saucepan and stir in 1 cup crunchy peanut butter (or 1 cup of crisped rice cereal) until blended. Remove from the heat and fold in 2 cups mini marshmallows.

Spread the mixture into a 9- by 13-inch greased baking pan. Cover and chill until the candy firms up (about 10 to 15 minutes). Cut into 1½-inch squares. Makes 4 dozen.

Prep time: 15 minutes Cooking time: 15 minutes

Index

Photographers

Stylists

Grapefruit Gal, page 21

Also from **FamilyFun**

FamilyFun Magazine: a creative guide to all the great things families can do together. For subscription information, call 800-289-4849.

FamilyFun Cookbook: a collection of more than 250 irresistible recipes for you and your kids, from healthy snacks to birthday cakes to dinners everyone in the family will enjoy (Disney Editions, $24.95).

FamilyFun Parties: a complete party planner featuring 100 celebrations for birthdays, holidays, and every day (Disney Editions, $24.95).

FamilyFun Birthday Cakes: a batch of 50 recipes for creative party treats (Disney Editions, $10.95).

FamilyFun Boredom Busters: 365 games, crafts, and activities for every day of the year (Disney Editions, $24.95).

FamilyFun Vacation Guide Series: take the vacation your family will remember with our guidebooks, covering New England, Florida and the Southeast, the Mid-Atlantic, the Great Lakes, the Southwest, and California and Hawaii.

FamilyFun.com: get ideas for snacks and introduce your child to the joys of cooking with more than 2,000 recipes in Recipe Finder. Visit www.familyfun.com/recipes